Mapping America:

A Guide to Historical Geography

Second Edition

Volume 1

Ken L. Weatherbie
Del Mar College

LONGMAN

An Imprint of Addison Wesley Longman, Inc.

New York • Reading, Massachusetts • Menlo Park, California • Harlow, England
Don Mills, Ontario • Sydney • Mexico City • Madrid • Amsterdam

Mapping America: A Guide to Historical Geography, Second Edition, Volume I.

Copyright © 1998 Longman Publishers USA, a division of Addison Wesley Longman, Inc.

ISBN: 0-321-00487-6

VG

98 99 00 01 02 9 8 7 6 5 4

Mapping America

CONTENTS

Preface

Preface

Mapping America: A Guide to Historical Geography is designed to provide a review of American geography and an introduction to the important role that the topography and geography of this continent has played in the history of the United States.

This workbook presents the basic geography of the United States—the places and river systems— so that students can place the history of the United States into spatial perspective. Sites and names serve as reference points for the rest of American history; unless one is very clear that Charleston is in South Carolina and Charlestown is in Massachusetts, some parts of the Revolutionary War can be quite confusing. A secondary objective of this workbook is to teach, and reinforce through practice, reading visual material as historical documents. The reference maps included here may be analyzed and interpreted much like a primary textual source—a speech or a letter—in order to glean information about the past. The third objective is to connect these maps to the historical period under consideration.

Keep the following two questions in mind while working on the exercises in this workbook.

From what point of view is the map drawn? Maps are drawn from one perspective or another. For example, each country usually puts itself in the middle of a world map. Think of how accustomed we are to seeing the Europe and the United States right smack in the middle of the world and how odd it would seem to have Australia in the center. Maps of the United States usually show Texas at the bottom, California on the left, and Maine on the right. They could just as well show Texas at the top—but that would look upside down. All map, like all documents, reflect choices about what is more important and what is less important.

Furthermore, one must remember that maps are always inadequate representations of geography-- no two-dimensional image can ever fully and accurately reproduce the three-dimensional sphere of the earth. Traditionally, map makers have used a modification of the Mercator projection in which the earth is projected into a cylinder. This type of projection is very distorted, however, particularly in that the areas around the poles appear to actually be much larger than they are (Greenland isn't really that big). The Mercator projection is only truly accurate in estimating areas and distances close to the equator.

What scale is shown on the map? As the shortcomings of the Mercator projection show, maps can be deceptive so scale is vitally important. If a map doesn't have a scale indicating how many inches (or centimeters) represent how many miles (or kilometers), compare it to another map. Are there differences? Remember how much bigger the western American states are than most eastern states, for example, or how small Europe really is as opposed to the other continents. Scale can also be very important to notice in historical maps of demographics, or population growth—a large city in 1750 isn't in the same ballpark as a large city in 1997 although maps may portray them as such.

The maps in this workbook are divided up into three sections, each with a brief introduction setting the context for the map exercise. On the opposing pages are questions in three categories:

Mapping America presents labeling and drawing exercises designed to review basic locations and spatial relationships.

Reading the Map includes a set of fill-in-the-blank questions that can be answered by studying the outline map and your textbook(s).

Interpreting the Map poses a series of general questions connecting geography with the historical era under consideration.

Text references and answers to the fill-in-the-blank and interpretive questions are provided in the back of this book.

It is our hope that *Mapping America* will improve your ability to read and interpret maps and will help you better understand and appreciate American history.

CHAPTER 1

THE PHYSICAL AND POLITICAL SETTING

The North American continent is an essential factor in the history of the American people. This is vital to the understanding of the history of the United States to understand the physiographical features of its land– its topography, climate, vegetation, and soils. The natural environment has played important roles in shaping the settlement, culture, and political life of the United States.

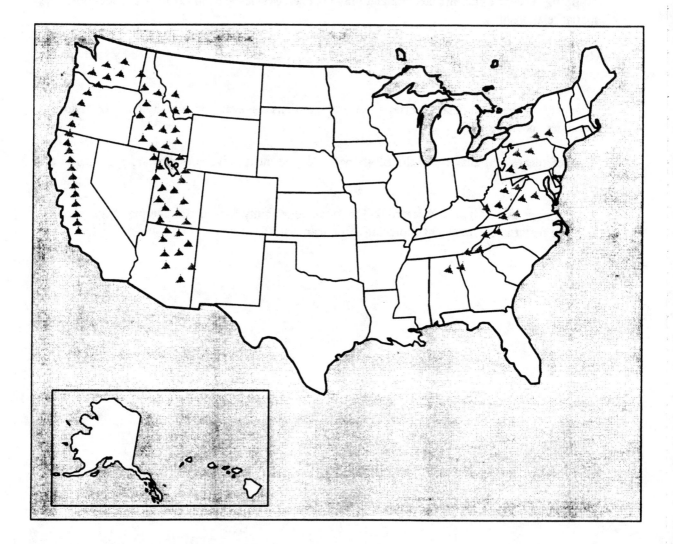

CHAPTER 1

MAPPING AMERICA

1. Label: Cascade Mountains, Sierra Nevada, Great Basin, Rocky Mountains, Great Plains, Appalachian Mountains, Atlantic Coastai Plain;.
2. Label: Mississippi River, Ohio River, Rio Grande, Columbia River, St. Lawrence River, each of the five Great Lakes, Great Salt Lake, Chesapeake Bay.
3. Draw light lines to designate, then label: 70th, 100th, and 125th meridians; 25th and 50th parallels.

READING THE MAP

1. Name two states that contain portions of the Cascade Mountains or Sierra Nevada.

   _____ _____

2. Name two states whose western borders are formed by the Mississippi River. _____

   _____

3. Name two states whose northern borders are formed by one or more of the Great Lakes.

   _____ _____

4. Name three states that contain a portion of the Rocky Mountains. _____

   _____ _____

5. Name three states that contain a portion of the Appalachian Mountains. _____

   _____ _____

6. Name three states that contain a portion of the Atlantic Coastal Plain. _____

   _____ _____

7. Name three states that contain a portion of the Great Plains. _____

   _____ _____

8. Name two states, portions of which lie within the Great Basin. _____

   _____

9. Between what lines of latitude and longitude lay the forty-eight contiguous states of the United States?
   _____ and _____ latitude; _____ and _____ longitude

INTERPRETING THE MAP

1. North America has been settled primarily from the water. What natural obstacles have Americans encountered in their movement from coast to coast?
2. What significant climactic and topographic differentiation occurs near 100° W longitude?
3. How did the physical characteristics of the continent affect settlement patterns, exploration routes, and transportation systems?
4. How were Native American groups distinguished and affected by the environments in the areas where they lived?
5. How did the natural environment influence the relationships between Native American groups and Europeans? When did the environment act to the Native American's advantage?
6. What group of states appear to have their borders defined by irregular natural features and which by symmetrical land-survey lines? How did this happen?

CHAPTER 2

DISCOVERY AND EXPLORATION

The sixteenth and seventeenth centuries were the great era of European global exploration. Spurred by the prospects of fame and wealth, adventurers mapped the oceans, established new trade routes, and circumnavigated the globe. These early seafarers were followed by soldiers and settlers who established colonies and empires in the Americas, as well as around the world. In the majority of contacts on this continent and elsewhere, the native groups these explorers encountered were devastated not only by superior military forces but also through the impact of diseases introduced by the European colonists.

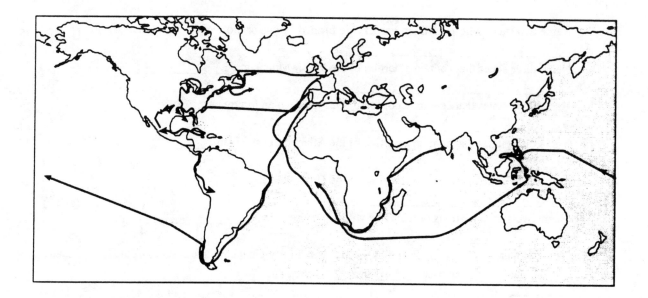

CHAPTER 2

1. Label: Pacific, Atlantic, and Indian Oceans; Caribbean Sea; Gulf of Mexico; Cape of Good Hope; Hudson Bay; Cape Horn.
2. Use a dot to locate, then label: Mexico City, Havana, Lima, Panama City, Santa Fe, St. Augustine.
3. Label: Newfoundland, Labrador, Greenland, Iceland, Cuba, Nova Scotia, Hispaniola.
4. Label: North America, South America, Europe, Africa, England, France, Spain, Portugal, India.
5. Label the routes of exploration of: Dias, Magellan, Cabot, Verrazzano, Coronado, de Soto, La Salle.
6. Label the predominant Native American regional groups in North America at the time of the initial European contacts.

READING THE MAP

1. _____, while sailing for Portugal, was the first European to round the Cape of Good Hope.
2. _____ rounded Cape Horn while sailing for Spain.
3. A Venetian sailor named _____ reconnoitered the coasts of Labrador and Newfoundland for England.
4. A Tuscan, with a French crew, _____ made the longest exploration to that point of what is now the east coast of the United States—from Cape Fear in North Carolina to the Penobscott river in Maine.
5. _____ and _____ simultaneously explored what are now the southwest and southeast regions of the United States.
6. _____ was the French explorer who first descended the entire Mississippi River Valley.
7. Francisco Pizarro's expedition originated from _____, on it he conquered and devastated the _____ in what is now _____.
8. The 1494 treaty that divided the New World into Spanish and Portuguese hemispheres was the

   _____.
9. Hernán Cortes's expedition ended in _____, called _____ by its inhabitants. He established his brutal reputation after triumphing over the _____, who had already been decimated by _____.
10. Florida was settled by _____, the governor of Puerto Rico who landed there in 1513 and was killed in 1521 by Native Americans resisting his attempts to colonize them and take them as slaves.

INTERPRETING THE MAP

1. What geographical factor helps explain why Portugal, Spain, France, and England dominated Atlantic seafaring in the sixteenth century?
2. Why was Brazil an exception to Spanish dominance in the conquest and colonization of Central and South America and the Caribbean?
3. Why did most of the sixteenth-century seafaring expeditions sail north or south of what is now the east coast of the United States?
4. Discuss how the biological exchange during the settlement and exploration periods—in which diseases, animals, and plants were traded across the continents en masse for the first time–may have been affected by the physical environment of the Americas, the routes of the explorers, and the settlement patterns of the European colonists.

CHAPTER 3

ENGLAND'S NORTH AMERICAN COLONIES IN 1700

By 1700, the English had been settled in North America for nearly a century and had established twelve separate colonies along the East Coast. France settled to the north and west, and Spain to the south and west. Stretched along a vast and varied terrain, the English colonies developed regional peculiarities in their cultures, social rituals, politics, and relationships with the mother country. In addition to the English, French, and Spanish, many millions of Native Americans lived along the eastern seaboard and had lived there long before the European's arrival.

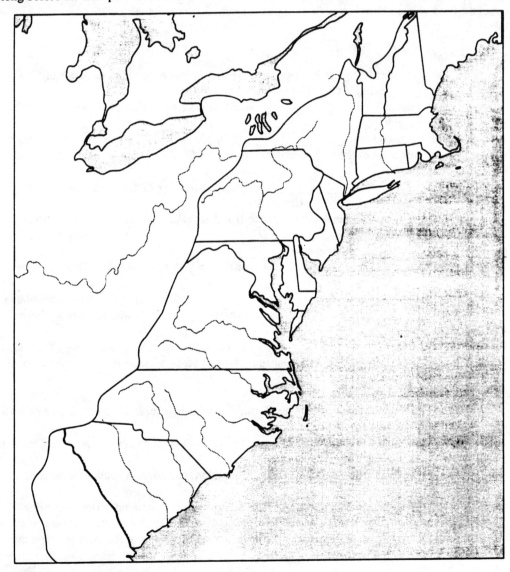

CHAPTER 3

MAPPING AMERICA

1. Label: New York, Massachusetts, South Carolina, East and West Jersey, Maryland, Connecticut, North Carolina, Delaware, Rhode Island, Pennsylvania, New Hampshire, Virginia, Georgia.
2. Locate by placing a dot, then label: Jamestown, Boston, Philadelphia, Providence, Salem, Charleston, Newport, New York City, Plymouth, Williamsburg.
3. Label: Cape Cod, Long Island, Chesapeake Bay, Connecticut River, Delaware River, Potomac River, James River, Hudson River, Susquehanna River.
4. Mark the areas where four major conflicts of the early colonial period took place: King Philip's War, Bacon's Rebellion, King William's War, and the Southern Indian Wars.
5. Mark the locations of the following Native American groups: the Powhatan, the Susquehannock, the Wampanoags, the Abenaki, the Narragansett, the Pequots, the Mohegans, the Tuscarora, the Delaware, the Cherokee, the Catawba, the Mohawks. Distinguish the Algonquian and the Iroquoian language groups.

READING THE MAP

1. The Potomac River forms the border between _____ and _____.
2. The Connecticut River is the western boundary of _____.
3. The Delaware River forms the western boundary of _____.
4. The smallest colony was _____, and was located just east of the colony of _____ and south of _____.
5. The first permanent English settlement was _____, located on the northern bank of the _____ River near _____ Bay.
6. The thirteenth colony, founded over fifty years after the twelfth, was _____, located south of the _____ River.
7. What three major rivers drained the middle colonies? _____, _____, _____

INTERPRETING THE MAP

1. What is the relationship between rivers and the locations of major towns and cities in colonial America? Account for this relationship.
2. Through the seventeenth century, the English colonies in North America maintained closer and more constant contact with England than they did with one another. Explain how this was influenced by the geography, environment, and transportation systems of eastern North America.
3. Speculate on how the environment in the New England, Chesapeake, middle, and southern colonies influenced their economies and social structures.
4. Using a detailed contemporary atlas, look up some of the place names from early New England on a map of England. Speculate about some of the choices early settlers made about what to name their new homes.

CHAPTER 4

THE ATLANTIC SLAVE TRADE

Between 1400 and 1800, European traders transported more than 10 million Africans to be slaves in the Americas. Thousands of Africans died on the long and tortuous "middle passage" across the Atlantic, but most survived to be enslaved in the British, French, Spanish, and Portuguese colonies. The majority were young men, destined to work on the sugar plantations of Latin America, but over a third of a million of them came to British North America, where they profoundly affected the colonies' economic, political, and social development. The slave trade was originally dominated by the Portuguese, whose sway over the industry was challenged by both the Dutch and English in the sixteenth century.

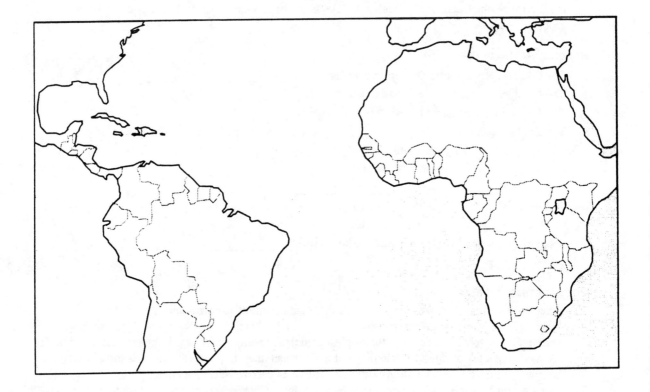

CHAPTER 4

MAPPING AMERICA

1. Label: North America, the West Indies, Brazil, New Spain, Africa, Madeira Island.
2. Label: Liberia, Ivory Coast, Ghana, Nigeria, Senegal.
3. Draw light line boundaries to show the West African cultures of: Ashanti, Yoruba, Ibo, Mandinkae, Mossi, and Hausa.
4. Label: Sahara Desert; Gulf of Guinea; Niger River; Grain, Gold, and Slave Coasts.
5. Draw a bold line to show the ancient empire of Ghana.

READING THE MAP

1. What role did Madeira play in the slave trade? _____

   _____

2. Match the native African culture group to the modern African nation with which it generally corresponds:

   a. Ibo – _____   c. Yoruba – _____

   b. Ashanti – _____   d. Mandingo – _____

3. Match the European-defined African "coast" to the modern African nation in which it is located:

   a. Grain Coast – _____   c. Gold Coast – _____

   b. Ivory Coast – _____   d. Slave Coast – _____

4. The peak period for slave importation to British North America was _____.
5. By the eighteenth century, African Americans (mostly slaves) made up almost fifty percent of the population of the _____ in what is now the United States.

INTERPRETING THE MAP

1. Why might the Portuguese have dominated the early African slave trade?
2. What geographical reality helps explain why relatively few African slaves were taken to the mainland colonies of British America?
3. What fact helps explain why the Atlantic slave trade changed from a small trickle to a major population shift after 1600? What other reasons might have caused some of the ebbs and flows in the slave trade?
4. What effect may it have had that the slaves brought to the Americas came from such a vast region of West Africa? Discuss the differences and similarities in the environments the slaves left in Africa and found in the Americas.

CHAPTER 5

THE STRUGGLE FOR THE CONTINENT

Between 1689 and 1763, England and France and their respective allies fought four wars known in the British colonies as the King William's War, Queen Anne's War, King George's Wars, and the French and Indian Wars, each of which had significant ramifications in their American colonies. In the first three of these wars, fighting in the colonies was peripheral to the main combat in Europe. But much of the French and Indian War was fought in the rugged terrain of North America, and the war evolved into a struggle for control of the continent. The outcome of this war in 1763 was decisive and in many ways contributed to the coming of the American Revolution.

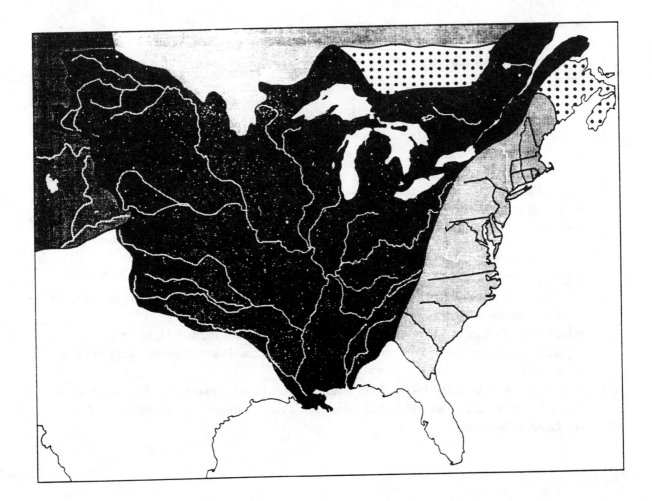

CHAPTER 5

1. Label: Mississippi, St. Lawrence, and Ohio Rivers; Lakes Superior, Michigan, Huron, Erie, and Ontario.
2. Locate with a dot, then label: Montreal, Quebec City, Albany, New Orleans, Boston, Port Royal, Ft. Duquesne, Ft. Niagara, Louisbourg.
3. Label: Spanish Florida, New France, French Louisiana.
4. Draw bold line boundaries to indicate, then label: North American territory held respectively by Spain, Britain, and France *after* the Peace of Paris of 1763.

READING THE MAP

1. Most French forts in North America were located on the extensive drainage system of the
   _____ River.
2. In which region of British North America was most of the fighting conducted in the colonial wars with France? _____
3. What were the two key French colonial cities usually targeted by British forces in the colonial wars?

   _____ _____
4. What key French fort, guarding the entry to New France, did the British capture in 1758?

   _____
5. What French fort eventually became the site of the city of Pittsburgh? _____
6. The building of what French fort directly contributed to provoking the French and Indian War?

   _____
7. Which French fort was "the critical link in the system of forts that joined the French inland empire with the Atlantic"? _____

INTERPRETING THE MAP

1. How did the French pattern of settlement in North America contribute to French settlers having friendlier relations with Native Americans than did English settlers?
2. Why did the New England colonies suffer most in the colonial wars with France?
3. What geographical fact contributed to the decision to charter the founding of the Georgia colony in 1732?

CHAPTER 6

THE AMERICAN REVOLUTION

The American Revolution engaged the armies of Britain, France, and the newly declared independent United States. For both the Americans and British it was a difficult and bloody conflict—it remains America's second-longest war. The physical geography of the North American continent played a key role in the strategy and campaigning of both sides in the war. Ultimately, the terrain offered the most advantages to George Washington's Continental Army and the colonial militia. In addition to gaining the United States' independence from Britain, the war also resulted in significant transfers of North American territory.

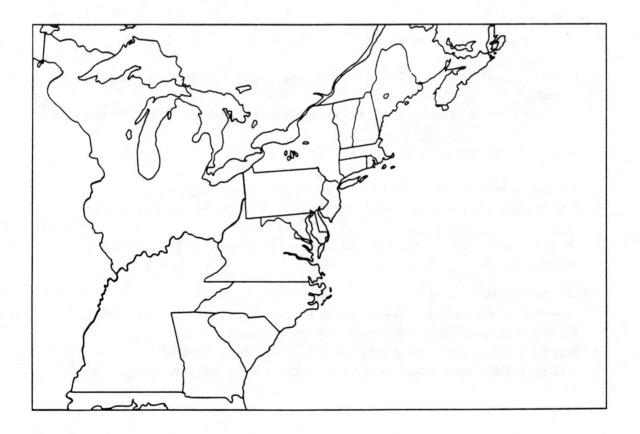

CHAPTER 6

1. Locate with a dot, then label: Boston, New York, Philadelphia, Halifax, Valley Forge.
2. Locate with an X, then label, noting also the dates of battle: Saratoga, Yorktown, Lexington, Concord, Bunker Hill, Brooklyn Heights, Princeton, Trenton, Charleston, Brandywine, Camden, King's Mountain, Germantown, Guilford Courthouse, Cowpens.
3. Draw a bold line tracing the Proclamation Line of 1763.
4. Use varied shadings to identify, then label these territorial claims in North America following the Treaty of Paris of 1783: (1) original thirteen states of the United States, (2) United States territory, (3) British territory, (4) Spanish territory.

READING THE MAP

1. When British troops left Boston in 1776 they went to _____, and when they invaded New York later that year they came from _____ .
2. How are the locations of American battles with Native Americans during the Revolutionary War geographically related to American battles with the British Army? _____
   _____
3. In what colony did Revolutionary War fighting begin in 1775? _____
4. What three states saw most military campaigning in 1776–1777? _____
   _____ _____
5. What three states saw most military campaigning in 1780–1781? _____
   _____ _____
6. Which side found it easier to utilize the Atlantic to move its troops and supplies in the Revolutionary War? _____

INTERPRETING THE MAP

1. What geographical considerations helped the British decide to relocate their headquarters to New York in 1776?
2. What geographical considerations helped the British decide to shift the area of their campaigning to the south after 1778?
3. What geographical features of the North American continent influenced the way the Revolutionary War was fought and helped determine its outcome?

CHAPTER 7

LAND ACQUISITIONS, 1782–1830

From the end of the Revolution to the 1830s, the United States acquired vast new territories from a number of sources. Land concessions by several of the original states to the new Confederation's government; the purchase of Louisiana from France; and treaties with Spain, Britain, and Native American groups all contributed to the nation's territorial growth in these years. Acquisition of these lands, and their survey, and sale, and settlement were primary concerns of the national government in the first half of the nineteenth century.

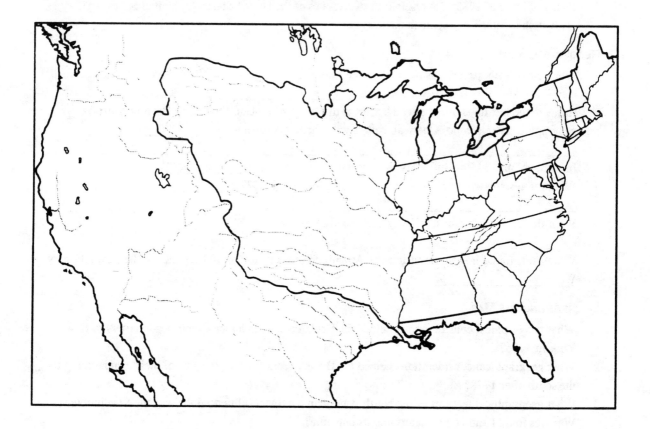

CHAPTER 7

MAPPING AMERICA

1. Use a variety of shadings to identify, then label: Northwest Territory, land ceded to the national government by the original states, Louisiana Purchase territory, West Florida, Oregon Country, land sold to the United States by Spain, land ceded the United States by Native Americans before 1830.
2. Label: Ohio, Mississippi, and Missouri Rivers; Appalachian and Rocky mountains.

READING THE MAP

1. The largest land cession made by a single state to the national government the 1780s was made by

    _____.
2. Most of the land cessions made by Indian tribes between 1750 and 1783 were south of the
    _____ River and west of the _____ Mountains; most of those made between 1784 and 1810 were north of the _____ River and west of the
    _____ River.
3. The Sac and Fox Indians made their land cessions to the United States in the years between _____ and _____. The Choctaw and Creek Indians made their land cessions in the years between _____ and _____.
4. The Louisiana Purchase extended the Untied States' territorial claims from the _____ River west to the _____ Mountains.
5. The United States first gained access to the Gulf of Mexico when it acquired _____.
6. Following the purchase of Louisiana, the United States had borders with _____ territory in the south and west, and _____ territory in the west and north.

INTERPRETING THE MAP

1. Why are the Land Ordinances of 1785 and 1787 considered the most notable accomplishments of the Confederation? What did these ordinances do?
2. Why is the Louisiana Purchase characterized as a "magnificent acquisition that would profoundly shape the nation's future"? What did the Purchase accomplish?
3. Research a historical atlas of the United States to determine how, before 1830, the United States acquired East and West Florida, the Red River Basin, and a claim to the Oregon Country.
4. Research and discuss the different land use patterns among Spanish, Dutch, English, and French settlers and how they affected social and political developments in different communities. Contrast these with the land-use patterns imposed by the Land Ordinance of 1785.

CHAPTER 8

ROUTES TO THE WEST, 1800–1860

Americans have always been a mobile people. Almost from the earliest settlements, Americans began moving west away from the Atlantic coast to the Appalachians, to the Mississippi, and on to the Pacific Coast. Over time, several beaten paths became the common roads and trails that wave upon wave of pioneers followed to the West and to the new opportunities they hoped it would offer. However, these Americans did not come upon an untouched land: the Spanish and the French had already established a presence in the middle and the western parts of North America, where their influence is still felt today, and Native American groups continued to both resist and grudgingly adapt to white settlement and invasion of their lands.

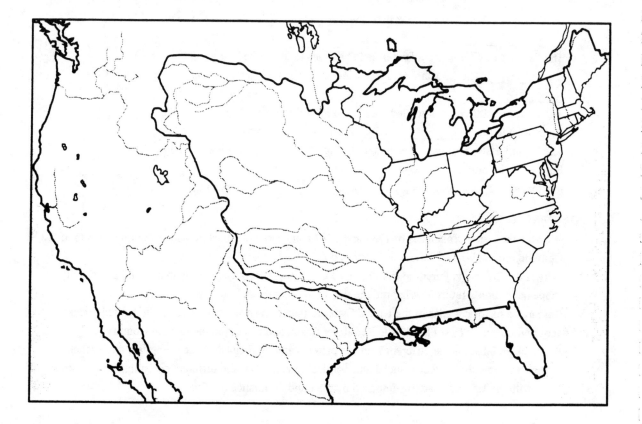

CHAPTER 8

MAPPING AMERICA

1. Label: Appalachian, Rocky, and Cascade Mountains, Sierra Nevada; Mississippi, Ohio, Columbia, Hudson, Missouri, Red, Platte, and Arkansas Rivers; Rio Grande; Cumberland Gap; South Pass; Great Salt Lake

2. Locate with a dot, then label: Buffalo, Pittsburgh, Nashville, Cincinnati, Louisville, Natchez, St. Louis, Santa Fe, Independence, Nauvoo

3. Draw a bold line tracing each of the following: Lancaster Turnpike, National Road, Wilderness Road, Natchez Trace, Forbes Road, Cumberland Gap Road, Hudson-Mohawk Route, Oregon Trail, California Trail, Mormon Trail, Santa Fe Trail

4. Use broken lines to locate, then label the routes: of Meriwether Lewis and William Clark, and of Zebulon Pike.

5. Locate the paths of the Cherokee, Creek, Seminole, and Chickasaw removals.

READING THE MAP

1. What three roads led into the trans-Appalachian Northwest? _____

   _____ _____

2. What road led into the Appalachian South? _____

3. What route would have been the best choice for travel from the mid–Atlantic Coast to Pittsburgh? _____ to Cincinnati? _____ to Nashville? _____

4. Lewis and Clark's routes to and from the Pacific Coast generally followed what three rivers?

   _____ _____ _____

5. Zebulon Pike explored the upper reaches of what three rivers? _____

   _____ _____

6. The Oregon Trail generally followed what three rivers to the Pacific? _____

   _____ _____

7. The Mormon Trek and Oregon Trail shared what route through the Rockies? _____

8. The early stretch of both the Mormon Trek and Oregon Trail followed the same route along the _____ River.

INTERPRETING THE MAP

1. What made Independence, Missouri the gathering and "jumping off" place for pioneers heading west on the overland trails?

2. What geographical considerations made the Mormons decide to settle near the Great Salt Lake?

3. Why was traversing the first half of the Oregon Trail easier on the pioneers than the second?

4. The movement of Europeans westward caused tremendous displacement of and conflict with Native Americans, many of whom migrated themselves. Some groups, such as the Mohawk moved north, while some such as the Seneca settled onto reservations, others, like the Cherokee were forcibly moved west and very few were able to stand their ground. Discuss the impact of Native Americans on the movement westward and the impact of the changing natural environment on the Native Americans.

CHAPTER 9

THE WAR OF 1812

After suffering through nearly two decades of British violations of America's neutral rights, Congress declared war on Britain in June, 1812. The War of 1812 raged for nearly three years without a military decision. As it did in the American Revolution, the geography of North America influenced the campaigns of the war and helped determine its outcome.

CHAPTER 9

1. Label: each of the five Great Lakes, St. Lawrence River, Lake Champlain, Chesapeake Bay.
2. Locate with an X, then label noting also the dates of battle: New Orleans, Washington, D.C., Detroit, York (Toronto), Baltimore, Pensacola, Buffalo, Horseshoe Bend, Ft. Dearborn, Tippecanoe.

READING THE MAP

1. Near what modern city did the first major battle of the War of 1812 occur? _____
2. Near what modern city did the last major battle associated with the War of 1812 occur?

   _____
3. In 1812–1813, the United States' strategy was to try to invade Canada at three points. What modern cities are near those three points of invasion? _____ _____

   _____
4. In 1814, the British strategy was to invade the United States at four points. What modern cities are near those four points of invasion? _____ _____

   _____ _____
5. Aside from its blockade of the Atlantic, the British navy conducted operations on several bodies of water in North America. Name three of them. _____ _____

   _____
6. Which battle of the War of 1812 signaled "an end to Indian resistance in the Old Northwest"?

   _____
7. Which battle of the War of 1812 "broke the back of Indian defenses in the South"?

   _____
8. Ft. Dearborn was located on the site of what modern city? _____

INTERPRETING THE MAP

1. What geographical fact explains why the Battle of New Orleans was fought after the treaty ending the War of 1812 was already signed?
2. Look at the locations of the battles in the War of 1812. Why were there no battles between British and American troops in the interior of North America between the Great Lakes and the Gulf of Mexico?
3. At least one military historian criticizes the American plan for the invasion of Canada in 1812–1813 for ignoring a simple geographical reality, which, if realized, might have led to victory at Montreal and American control of Canada. What was that geographical reality?

CHAPTER 10

THE MISSOURI COMPROMISE

As the nation expanded westward in the early nineteenth century, it had to decide whether the Constitution allowed slavery in the territories. The first confrontation with this issue came in 1819–1820 when the citizens of Missouri Territory petitioned to enter the Union as a slave state. Before any decision was made, congressional debates demonstrated how dangerously divisive the issue of territorial expansion and slavery could, and would be.

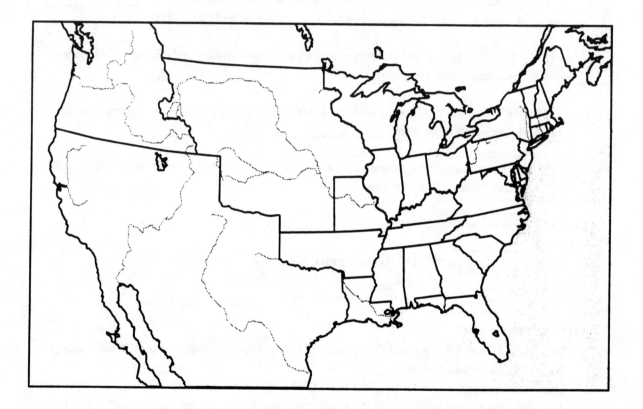

CHAPTER 10

1. Label:
    a. Arkansas, Florida, and Michigan Territories; Unorganized Territory.
    b. Missouri, Kentucky, Virginia, Ohio, Indiana, Illinois, and Maine.
    c. Mississippi and Ohio Rivers.
    d. 36° 30′ N latitude.
2. Draw a double line along the boundary between the free and slave *states* in the Union in 1819.
3. Shade with horizontal lines the free *territories* in the Union in 1821. Shade with vertical lines the *territories* open to slavery in 1821.

READING THE MAP

1. How many free states were in the Union in 1821? _____ How many slave states? _____
2. What territory was opened to slavery by the Missouri Compromise? _____ What territory was closed to slavery by the Missouri Compromise? _____
3. What free state was admitted to the Union in 1820 to offset the admission of Missouri as a slave state? _____
4. What natural geographical feature formed a lengthy portion of the boundary between free and slave *states* in 1819? _____
5. What formed the boundary between free and slave *territory* in 1820? _____

INTERPRETING THE MAP

1. What geographical limitations of the Missouri Compromise meant that in the future the fate of slavery in United States territories would have to be debated again?
2. What geographical considerations lay behind the placement of the line dividing free and slave territory in the Missouri Compromise?
3. Look at your map. Compare the size of the territory closed to slavery by the Missouri Compromise to the size of the territory open to slavery. Why do you suppose southern congressmen were willing to accept the Missouri Compromise with such an obvious disparity of the distribution of real estate?

CHAPTER 11

THE ANTEBELLUM SOUTH AND SLAVERY

After 1820, cotton became the most profitable crop in the southern economy. The increased production made possible by Eli Whitney's cotton gin, the mobility of slave labor, and the incessant quest of southern whites for fertile soils pushed the southern frontier westward into Texas by 1860. In this expanding culture of King Cotton, slavery embedded itself ever more firmly in the southern way of life.

CHAPTER 11

1. Draw a bold line to indicate the boundary separating those states whose slave populations on the eve of the Civil War were *more* than 40 percent of their total populations (label these states the Lower South) from those states whose slave population was *less* than 40 percent of the total population (label these states the Upper South). Draw borders showing where the South had the heaviest concentration of slaves in 1860. Shade this area with horizontal lines.
2. Draw borders to show the areas in the South having the heaviest concentration of
   a. cotton production. Shade this area with vertical lines.
   b. rice production. Lightly shade this area with a pencil.
   c. tobacco production. Leave this area unshaded.

READING THE MAP

1. Name the states of the Lower South in 1860.

   _____ _____ _____

   _____ _____ _____

2. In 1860, what states showed the closest correspondence between the concentration of slaves and the highest levels of production of cotton, rice, and tobacco?

   cotton: _____ _____ _____

   rice: _____ _____

   tobacco: _____ _____

3. Draw a set of arrows on your map indicating the direction of the slave population's movement in the South from 1820 to 1860.

INTERPRETING THE MAP

1. What is a geographical explanation for the concentration of the cotton culture in the areas indicated on your map?
2. What major geographical features help account for the economic differences between the Upper and Lower South?
3. In the 1850s, some argued that slavery had reached its "natural limits." What did they mean by this assertion?

CHAPTER 12

SETTLING THE BOUNDARY WITH CANADA

In the 1840s, the United States finished defining its boundary with British Canada. Earlier, portions of the border had been drawn through the Great Lakes and from the Lake of the Woods to the Continental Divide, but that left unresolved gaps on either side of the continent and in its middle. Following negotiated settlements in 1842 and 1846, the United States–Canada boundary became well delineated and whole.

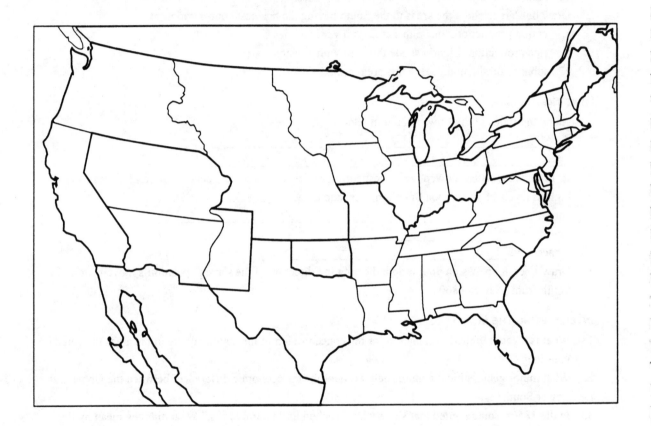

CHAPTER 12

MAPPING AMERICA

1. Label: Oregon Country, Canada, Louisiana Purchase territory unorganized in 1840, Vermont, New Hampshire, Maine.
2. Label: Lake of the Woods, Lake Superior, Puget Sound, Vancouver Island, 49° N latitude, Columbia River.
3. Draw a line tracing the Canadian boundary lines agreed to by the United States and Britain in 1842.
4. Draw a bold line tracing the boundary line agreed to by United States and Britain in the 1846 Oregon Settlement.

READING THE MAP

1. The Oregon Settlement established the United States–Canada boundary along the _____ parallel.
2. The Oregon Trail terminated at the confluence of what two rivers? _____

   _____
3. Had the boundary line agreed to in the Oregon Settlement been extended along the same line of latitude to the Pacific Ocean, the United States would have gained possession of the southern tip of

   _____.
4. In 1842, the United States and Britain reached an agreement on the eastern portion of the Canadian boundary that defined the northern limits of which two states? _____ and

   _____.
5. In 1842, the United States and Britain filled a gap in the Canadian boundary between the Great Lakes and Rocky Mountains by establishing a border that connected which two bodies of water?

   _____ _____

INTERPRETING THE MAP

1. What geographical consideration made the Oregon Settlement acceptable to President Polk even though it did not give the United States possession of all of Oregon to 54° 40′ N latitude, as he had promised in his presidential campaign in 1844?
2. What geographical feature made the establishment of the Canadian border just west of the Great Lakes of significant importance to the United States?
3. The Webster-Ashburton Treaty of 1842 defined the eastern portion of the United States–Canada boundary. Look up the treaty and determine what provoked its negotiation.

CHAPTER 13

TEXAS AND THE MEXICAN WAR

The 1840s was a decade of Manifest Destiny—Americans were determined to expand their nation's borders to the Pacific Ocean. This was accomplished by the annexation of the Republic of Texas in 1845 and by territorial conquest in a war with Mexico. As a result of these events, the United States acquired over 1.2 million square miles of new territory. Combined with the 1846 Oregon Settlement, these territorial additions made the United States a continental republic by the mid-nineteenth century.

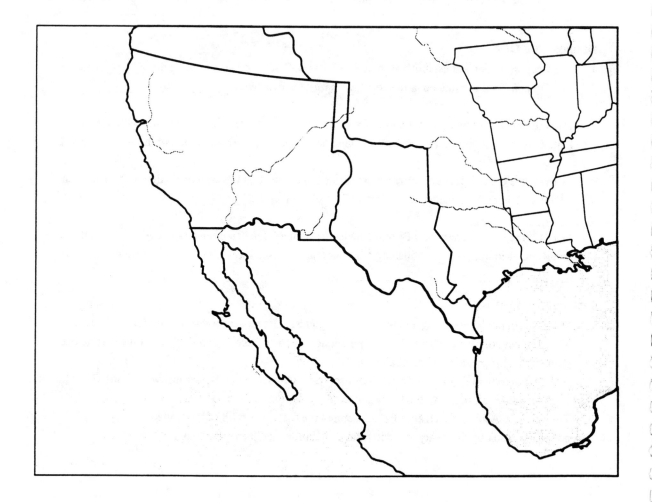

CHAPTER 13

1. Label: Arkansas, Red, Sabine, Gila, and Nueces Rivers, Rio Grande; 42° N latitude.
2. Locate with a dot, then label: Corpus Christi, Matamoros, Santa Fe, San Antonio, San Jacinto, New Orleans, San Diego, Ft. Leavenworth, Vera Cruz, Mexico City.
3. Draw a line indicating the boundaries of the Republic of Texas when it was annexed in 1845.
4. Draw a bold line indicating the boundaries of the territory Mexico ceded to the United States in the Treaty of Guadeloupe Hidalgo in 1848.
5. Use long-stemmed arrows to show the routes of the armies of generals Kearney, Taylor, and Scott during the Mexican War.

READING THE MAP

1. When annexed in 1845, the Republic of Texas was bounded on the east by the _____ River, on the north by the _____ and _____ Rivers, and on the west and south by the _____ .
2. The territory acquired by the United States in the Mexican Cession of 1845 was bounded on the east by the _____, and on the south by the _____ River.
3. In 1845, both Texas and the Mexican Cession territory had a northern boundary along the _____.
4. The disputed territory entered by General Taylor's army in 1846 that provoked war with Mexico lay between the _____ and _____.
5. General Kearney's army first captured the trade center at _____, then invaded

   _____.
6. General Scott's army made an amphibious landing and captured the Mexican coastal city of
   _____, then moved overland to capture _____.

INTERPRETING THE MAP

1. President Polk was willing to provoke war for California. What geographical consideration made American possession of California so desirable?
2. Besides the land itself, what natural features of the Cession Territory proved immensely valuable to the United States?
3. One additional territorial acquisition in the southwest in the mid-nineteenth century was the Gadsden Purchase. Where is it, who was Gadsden, and why was it acquired?

CHAPTER 14

THE COMPROMISE OF 1850 AND THE KANSAS-NEBRASKA ACT

The question of whether or not to allow slavery to expand into the Cession Territory acquired from Mexico in 1848 was answered in the Compromise of 1850. Popular sovereignty—allowing territorial residents to vote to determine the status of slavery among them—was adopted as the solution to this vexing problem. All seemed peaceful, but in 1854, when Senator Stephen A. Douglas applied popular sovereignty to the organization of the remaining unorganized Louisiana Purchase territory (renamed the Kansas-Nebraska Territory), he provoked a divisive political storm between North and South that significantly contributed to the coming civil war.

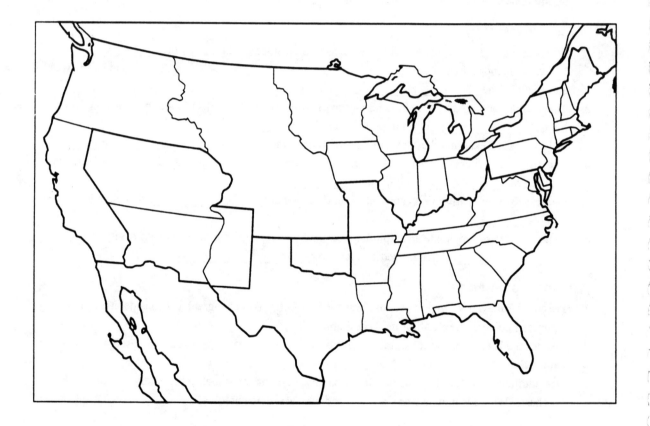

CHAPTER 14

1. Label: Utah Territory, New Mexico Territory, Kansas-Nebraska Territory, Indian Territory, California, Texas, 36° 30′ N latitude, 42° N latitude, 49° N latitude, Missouri River, Continental Divide.

2. Draw a bold line tracing the boundary separating the *free states and territories* from the *slave states and territories open to slavery* after the Compromise of 1850. Draw a double bold line indicating the same separation after the Kansas-Nebraska Act in 1854.

READING THE MAP

1. Between 1820 and 1850, slavery was not allowed to expand into U.S. territory north of _____ latitude. In 1850, it was made legal as far north as _____ latitude. In 1854, it became legal as far north as _____ latitude.

2. Which held the largest amount of national real estate: (a) free states and territories, or (b) slave states and territories open to slavery? Following the Compromise of 1850 it was _____ . Following the Kansas-Nebraska Act in 1854 it was _____ .

3. The Kansas-Nebraska Territory was bounded on the north by _____, on the west by the _____, on the south by _____, and on the east by the

   _____.

4. What free state joined the Union as part of the Compromise of 1850? _____

INTERPRETING THE MAP

1. Arguing from geographical considerations, why do you suppose the citizens of Missouri were especially interested in having the lower portion of the Kansas-Nebraska Territory (Kansas Territory) open to slavery?

2. In 1854 there was widespread agreement that slavery probably would not spread into the upper portion of the Kansas-Nebraska Territory (Nebraska Territory). What geographical explanation might there have been for this assumption? Given this, speculate on why northerners still insisted on a congressional ban on slavery's expansion rather than trust this "natural limits" argument.

3. In 1854, what geographical considerations prompted the effort to organize the Kansas-Nebraska Territory, which was widely considered the Great American Desert?

4. What environmental or agricultural distinctions may be found between the states that did and did not join the Confederacy?

CHAPTER 15

THE SECESSION CRISIS

When news spread that Republican Abraham Lincoln had won the presidential election of 1860, the Lower South seceded from the Union. After the firing on Ft. Sumter, four more slave states seceded and joined the new confederacy of southern slave states. Not all slave slaves joined the Confederate States of America, however, and the strategic location of these states would prove significant to the conduct and outcome of the Civil War.

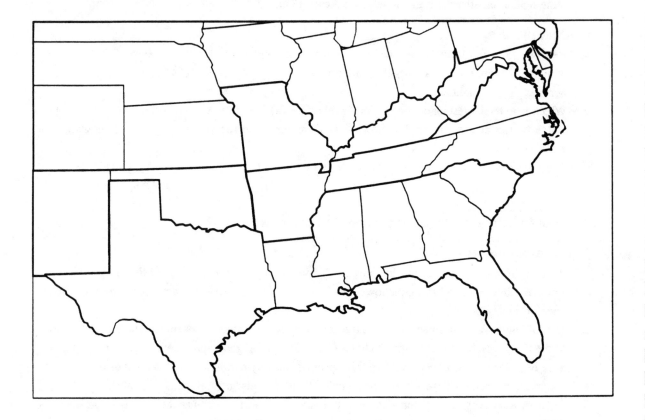

CHAPTER 15

1. Label: Ohio River, Mississippi River, Rio Grande, Richmond, Montgomery, Delaware, Maryland, Missouri, South Carolina, Louisiana, Virginia, Tennessee, Alabama, Kentucky, Texas, Mississippi, Georgia, Florida, Arkansas, North Carolina.
2. Draw a bold line that traces the border between the Union and the Confederacy.
3. Lightly shade those slave states that *did not* join the Confederacy in 1860–1861.

READING THE MAP

1. Before secession began, how many slaves states were in the Union? _____
2. The four slave states that did not join the Confederacy were _____,
    _____, _____, and _____.
3. The middle portion of the Confederacy's border with the Union was along the _____.
4. The trans-Mississippi states in the Confederacy (those west of the Mississippi River) were
    _____, _____, and _____.
5. The Confederacy was organized in the city of _____, but the capital was later moved
    to the city of _____.

INTERPRETING THE MAP

1. What geographical fact made it especially important that Texas joined the Confederacy?
2. What was the geographical importance of some slave states not joining the Confederacy?
3. Why do you suppose the South was geographically divided between a tier of states that seceded early, a second tier that seceded later, and a third tier that never did secede?

CHAPTER 16

THE CIVIL WAR

The Civil War, fought between 1861 and 1865, saw armies of unprecedented size engaged in bloody combat over a vast expanse of territory. Necessarily, the terrain influenced the grand strategies and field tactics of both sides. The maneuvering of armies, the transport of supplies, and the locations of battles were often determined by geographical factors. The Union victory was in part a result of its skillful consideration of the natural and constructed environments.

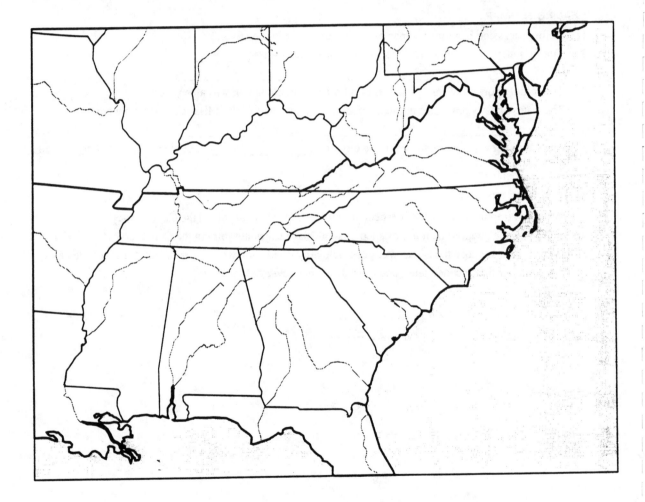

CHAPTER 16

1. Locate with an X, then label: Gettysburg, Richmond, Antietam, Bull Run, Vicksburg, New Orleans, Ft. Henry, Ft. Donelson, Shiloh, Atlanta, Chattanooga, Savannah, Washington, D.C., Appomattox.
2. Label: Ohio, Mississippi, Potomac, York, Cumberland, and Tennessee Rivers; Chesapeake Bay; Shenandoah Valley; Appalachian Mountains.
3. Draw an arrow to indicate the path of Sherman's March to the Sea.
4. Mark some of the major industrial areas, transportation routes, and urban areas in the United States before the Civil War.

READING THE MAP

1. The Peninsula campaign refers to the Union effort to seize _____ by invading it from the east along the peninsula formed by the _____ River and the _____ River.
2. The two major Civil War battles fought on Union soil were at _____ and _____.
3. The Union strategy to "divide and conquer" the Confederacy led to two lines of invasion. The first ran along the line of the _____ River, and the second along the _____ River. A third line of invasion, with an emphasis on "conquer" rather than "divide," was Sherman's march from _____ to _____.
4. The Union gained an important naval victory at the key southern port of _____ in 1862, but won virtual control of the Mississippi River only with the siege of _____, completed in mid-1863.
5. The first Union victories in the Civil War were at Forts _____ and _____ in western Tennessee, but their advance was blunted by Confederate defenses at _____.
6. The Union's resource advantages included _____, _____, and _____. The Confederate advantages included _____, _____, and _____.

INTERPRETING THE MAP

1. What geographical fact meant that a great deal of the fighting of the Civil War would be in northern Virginia?
2. Why was Tennessee a state of key strategic importance in the Civil War?
3. The Confederacy had no real navy. What geographical feature of the Confederacy blunted the impact of that deficiency?
4. Contrast the transportation and industrial systems in the North and South. How did locations of important transportation lines or industrial sites affect military strategy in the Civil War?

CHAPTER 17

RAILROADS AND NEW TRANSPORTATION SYSTEMS

The late nineteenth century saw an explosion of new railroads criss-crossing the American continent. A network of 30,000 miles of track in 1860 grew to include more than 190,000 miles of track by 1900. The early railroad system was a complex and inefficient one incorporating more than ten different rail gauges—meaning trains had to be unloaded and reloaded every time the track switched. After the Civil War, however, large monopolies began to dominate and buy up smaller railroads, and a standard gauge was adopted in 1886. The large railroads, financed by the government and the great corporations that managed them, spurred industrial development and helped introduce new economic and social patterns across the United States. They also drastically changed the American environment. More than anything, they opened up the West and closed the frontier.

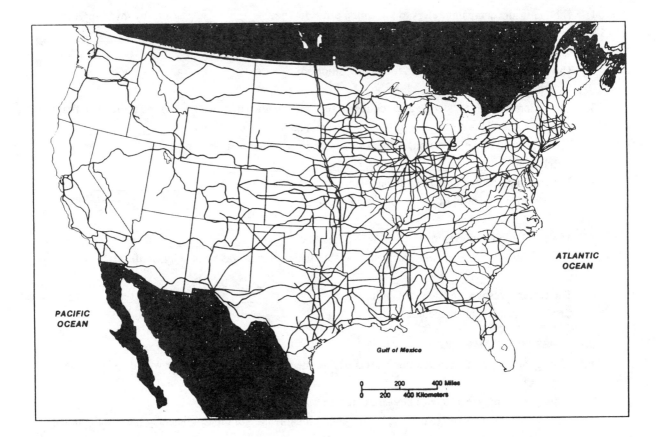

CHAPTER 17

1. Railroads were the second major new transportation system to emerge in 19th-century America. The first were the canals. Label the Erie and the Main Line Canals.
2. Using a highlighter, mark some of the major railroad systems of the late nineteenth century: the Union Pacific, the Central Pacific, the Northern Pacific, and the Southern Pacific Railroads.
3. Locate with a dot, then label some of the new industrial cities that the railroads made even more dominant: San Francisco, Denver, Chicago, St. Louis, Memphis, New York, Kansas City, and Charleston.
4. Indicate on the map the locations of some of the new mining and cattle production areas in the West.

READING THE MAP

1. One of the major conflicts in the early plans for a transcontinental railroad centered on where to put the railroad's eastern terminus; in Chicago, a city in a free state, or in a slave state such as Tennessee. During the Civil War, the Union Pacific railroad was begun with its eastern terminus at _____ and its western terminus at _____.
2. The Central Pacific and the Union Pacific Railroads met up at _____, near _____ in the state of _____.
3. The _____ ran from San Francisco and Los Angeles to New Orleans and was completed in 1883.
4. The transcontinental railroads were built by immigrants from _____ and _____.

INTERPRETING THE MAP

1. What was the effect of the opening of the trans-continental railroad on the economy and society of the American West?
2. How did the railroads adapt and influence the settlement and development patterns of the United States?
3. What were the geographical factors that made a transcontinental railroad difficult to finish? What were the social and political challenges to such a project?
4. Discuss the impact of the railroad on the environment of the West.

CHAPTER 18

TERRITORIAL EXPANSION TO THE CIVIL WAR

The United States grew by gradual acquisitions of territory from which, in time, new states were organized and admitted to the Union. These acquisitions were sometimes peacefully accomplished through negotiations with Native Americans and foreign nations, but other times were the spoils of war. By the end of the Civil War, the United States was a continental republic stretching from the Atlantic to the Pacific Oceans and from Canada to Mexico and the Gulf of Mexico.

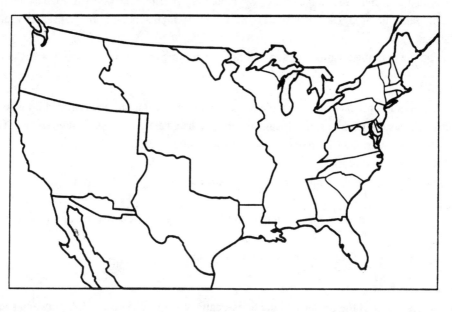

CHAPTER 18

1. Label: original thirteen states, Old Northwest, Louisiana Purchase territory, Texas, Mexican Cession territory, Oregon Country, Gadsden Purchase. Shade the territories acquired as a result of the Treaty of Paris of 1783 and the Adams-Onis Treaty (Transcontinental Treaty).
2. Mark some of the major Native American reservations in 1890, including those for the Hopi, Navajo, Ute, Apache, Crow, and Sioux.

READING THE MAP

1. List the original thirteen states. _____ _____

   _____ _____ _____ _____
   _____ _____ _____ _____
   _____ _____ _____

2. List five states whose lands include portions of the Old Northwest. _____

   _____ _____ _____ _____

3. Other than the original thirteen and those in the Old Northwest, list six states formed from territory acquired in the Treaty of Paris of 1783. _____ _____

   _____ _____ _____ _____

4. List nine states containing lands acquired in the Louisiana Purchase. _____

   _____ _____ _____ _____
   _____ _____ _____ _____

5. What state was admitted from territory acquired in the Transcontinental Treaty?

   _____

6. What state other than those of the original thirteen joined the Union without first having been a United States territory? _____

7. List three states containing lands gained in the Mexican Cession. _____

   _____ _____

8. List three states created from lands in the Oregon Country.

   _____ _____ _____

INTERPRETING THE MAP

1. In the process of transcontinental movement, Native American groups were pushed further westward. Discuss the impact of this on the development of the West.
2. Review the environmental differences and distinctions among the West, the plains states, and the eastern states. Discuss how these environmental differences might account for distinct social or political experiences. Is there a distinctive western character?

CHAPTER 19

RECONSTRUCTION

For a dozen years after the Civil War, the nation was engaged in the process of readmitting the former Confederate states into the Union. It was a slow, controversial, and, for some, painful process. Under Union aegis, the states of the Reconstruction South inaugurated Republican governments in the years immediately following the civil War. Republican power, however, was short-lived: it was not long before Southern white Democrats were able to retake state governments across the Confederacy and reassert conservative control, a process called "redemption." By the time of the Compromise of 1877, which ended Reconstruction, every Confederate state's government had been "redeemed."

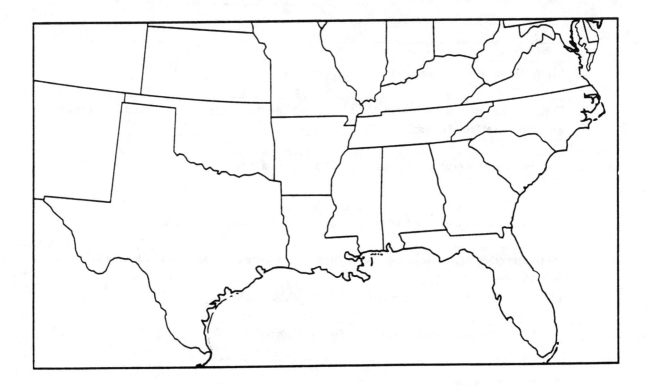

CHAPTER 19

1. Label each of the five military districts established in March 1867.
2. Indicate in each state the year that it was readmitted into the Union; also indicate the year each state was "redeemed" by conservative Democrats.

READING THE MAP
1. What was the first of the former Confederate states to be readmitted to the Union?
   _____

2. The Reconstruction Acts were passed in early 1867. Which state escaped the provisions of these laws?
   _____

3. Which two states spent the shortest time between readmission and redemption? _____
   _____

4. Which three states spent the longest time between readmission and redemption? _____
   _____ _____

5. Which state was readmitted with a conservative redeemer government already in power?
   _____

6. The Fifteenth Amendment was ratified in 1870. Which states had already been readmitted by then?
   _____ _____ _____ _____
   _____ _____ _____

7. Which three states were the last to elect redeemer governments? _____
   _____ _____

INTERPRETING THE MAP
1. In the 1867 Reconstruction Acts, why did Congress subdivide the former Confederacy geographically into five military districts?
2. What former Confederate states were most affected by the Compromise of 1877?
3. Why weren't the former Confederate states all readmitted at the same time?

CHAPTER 1: ANSWERS

THE PHYSICAL AND POLITICAL SETTING

READING THE MAP

1. Washington, Oregon, California, and Nevada
2. Wisconsin, Illinois, Kentucky, Tennessee, and Mississippi
3. Wisconsin, Michigan, Illinois, Indiana, Ohio, Pennsylvania, and New York
4. Washington, Idaho, Montana, Wyoming, Utah, Colorado, Arizona, and New Mexico
5. Pennsylvania, West Virginia, Maryland, Virginia, Kentucky, Tennessee, North Carolina, South Carolina, and Georgia
6. All states that border on the Atlantic Ocean or the Gulf of Mexico from Maine to Texas (The coastal plain along the Gulf of Mexico is an extension of the Atlantic Coastal Plain.): Maine, New Hampshire, Massachusetts, Rhode Island, Connecticut, New York, New Jersey, Pennsylvania, Delaware, Maryland, Virginia, North Carolina, South Carolina, Georgia, Florida, Alabama, Mississippi, Louisiana, and Texas.
7. Montana, North Dakota, South Dakota, Minnesota, Nebraska, Iowa, Missouri, Kansas, Oklahoma, and Texas
8. Wyoming, Oregon, Idaho, Nevada, Utah, Arizona, and New Mexico,
9. Approximately 24° N latitude (24th parallel) and 50° N latitude; approximately 68° W longitude (68th meridian) and 125° W longitude

INTERPRETING THE MAP

1. North America's geographical features generally run north to south. As settlers moved west they encountered in succession, the Appalachian and Allegheny Mountains, the Mississippi River, Rocky Mountains, and Sierra Nevada and Cascade Mountains.
2. Near 100° W longitude, the land becomes more elevated and there is a significant decline in annual rainfall and natural vegetation.
3. The physical characteristics of the North American continent significantly influenced settlement patterns, exploration routes, and transportation. In the early settlements east of the Appalachians, settlement followed two general patterns: in the Northeast, where the land was more wooded and not always arable, settlers tended to cluster near the coasts, The South was generally more hospitable to farming, and thus made plantations and a less-dense population feasible. As Americans moved westward, explorers first crossed the continent by following its rivers; keeping to the rivers usually assured them fresh water and game, as well as often provided routes through mountains. Where they could not follow rivers through mountains, they were forced to find passes. In turn, settlement of the West and the trade routes there took shape along the routes mapped by explorers, with cities and commerce centers established at the confluence of rivers or at mountain passes. The West's settlement, as that of the East, was also deeply affected by the arability of the land and natural resources available; for example, the relative scarcity of water and wood long delayed white settlement of the Great Plains.
4. The very distinct regional cultures of Native American groups are to a great extent attributable to the environments they evolved in. In the wooded East, Indian groups lived in more or less permanent villages, practicing varying combinations of agriculture and hunting and gathering from their

surrounding areas. With significantly less water and arable land available, the Plains Indians depended on the buffalo for food and developed a nomadic hunter-gatherer lifestyle, seasonally covering large areas of hunting territory. Native Americans in the Pacific Northwest lived similarly to their counterparts in the East, exploiting their region's rivers and woods for food. In the Southwest, groups like the Hopi and Pueblo formed agricultural communities around water sources.

5. America's natural environment was a profound influence on Native American and European relations. In the East and Northwest, where at first there appeared to be land enough to support the small groups of settlers and Native Americans, many Indian groups sought to coexist and trade with, and population grew and pushed the Indians off the lands. In the Plains , whites met with more hostility: resources were scarce, and the Plain Indian tribes lived in established yet often disputed territories, in a relative balance with one another and the environment. White settlements tipped that balance, encroaching on these territories and increasing competition for food and water. But at least at the outset, before disease, sheer numbers, and superior technology and military force took their toll, their various environments worked to the Natives' advantage in conflicts with the settlers. While the Indians knew well the lads around them, such environments were often alien to the whites.

6. The easternmost states have boundaries more often determined by natural features, while the western states have straight-line boundaries. This in part the result of the active role taken by the national government in surveying and planning for the introduction of new states created from the territories as the nation moved west.

CHAPTER 2: ANSWERS

DISCOVERY AND EXPLORATION

READING THE MAP
1. Bartolomeu Dias
2. Ferdinand Magellan
3. John Cabot
4. Giovanni da Verrazzano
5 Francisco Coronado; Hernando de Soto
6. René-Robert Cavalier, Sieur de La Salle (La Salle)
7. Panama City, Incas, Peru
8. Treaty of Tordesillas
9. Mexico City, Tenochitlan, Aztecs, smallpox
10. Ponce de Leon

INTERPRETING THE MAP
1. Just as the Italian states' location helped them dominate the Mediterranean sea lanes in the fifteenth century, Portugal, Spain, France, and England all capitalized on their locations fronting on the Atlantic Ocean to dominate seafaring to the New World.
2. The Pope's Demarcation Line, which divided the world between Portugal and Spain via the Treaty of Tordesillas in 1494 crossed the eastern tip of South America (approximately 48° W longitude), thus giving Portugal claim to the area that became Brazil.

3. The sixteenth century was an age of sailing ships; seafarers had to pay close attention to prevailing winds and ocean currents. The winds and currents flowing west from Europe carried seafarers to the Caribbean and South America or, by a northern route, to Greenland and Labrador. The prevailing winds and currents off the eastern coast of what is now the United States flow east and were used by seafarers to return to Europe. Additionally, these explores went north in their attempts to locate the fabled Northwest Passage to China.

4. The biological exchange during the age of exploration and settlement was virtually dictated by the physical environment of the Americas. The natural environment shaped exploration and trade routes and subsequent settlement patterns, and all exchanges of plants, animals, and diseased occurred in the contacts made along these routes. The results of those exchanges then either were brought back to Europe or spread out over the American continent(s) through broadening networks of biological contact. Furthermore, the environment influenced how far along those networks certain phenomena could progress: some plants or animals introduced by Europeans may not survive in particular American regions; some Native Americans could be resistant to certain European diseases (or vice versa).

CHAPTER 3: ANSWERS

ENLAND'S NORTH AMERICAN COLONIES IN 1700

READING THE MAP
1. Maryland and Virginia
2. New Hampshire
3. New Jersey
4. Rhode Island, Connecticut, Massachusetts
5. Jamestown, James, Chesapeake
6. Georgia, Savannah
7. Hudson, Delaware, Susquehanna

INTERPRETING THE MAP
1. The major towns and provincial capitals in colonial America were almost all located on rivers, and most were where those rivers meet to the sea. These coastal cities maintained contact with Europe and the mother country through commercial trade and served as ports of arrival and departure. Especially in the South, the rivers were navigable for some distance upstream and were for a long time major arteries of transportation.
2. The English colonies stretched over several hundred miles of forested terrain from New Hampshire to Georgia. Given the means of transportation available (foot and horseback) and the numerous rivers to cross, these were considerable distances to travel, thus inhibiting contact between the colonies. And as far as sea travel, given currents and winds, it was almost as easy to travel between the colonies and England as it was, for example, between Georgia and Massachusetts. But, perhaps the most important reason for the American colonies communicating better with England than with one another was that they were chartered to different owners pursuing diverse interests all based in Britain.

3. The New England colonies, located further north with a shorter growing season and plagued by rocky soils, turned to fishing and commerce as important bulwarks of their economy. In the Chesapeake and the South, the soils and climate favored plantation agriculture and these colonies focused on using slave labor to cultivate staple crops like tobacco and rice. The middle colonies were blessed with good soils and a moderate climate and grew surpluses of wheat and other foodstuffs for export. The Delaware, Susquehanna, and Hudson Rivers also gave the middle colonies ready access to their backcountry and the profitable fur trade with the Indians. Thus in northern and middle colonies and urban merchant culture with a budding middle class took shape while in the southern colonies a more rural and socially rigid system evolved.
4. Many of the names settlers chose for their new homes were taken from their towns and regions of origin in England, or else reflected their ideals (as in [Jeru]salem or Providence) or honored prominent figures (as in Amherst or Winthrop).

CHAPTER 4: ANSWERS

THE ATLANTIC SLAVE TRADE

READING THE MAP

1. Madeira was the first European overseas colony organized around slave labor.
2. a. Nigeria   c. Nigeria.
    b. Ghana   d. Senegal
3. a. Liberia   c. Ghana.
    b. Ivory Coast   d. Nigeria
4. 1761–1770.
5. Lower South

INTERPRETING THE MAP

1. The Portuguese were among the age of discovery's earliest navigators, and were the first to establish trade centers along Africa's west coast. Slaves, the Portuguese and many of their African partners were simply another commodity. Portugal also saw the utility of mass slave labor on its Madeira sugar plantations.
2. The harsher weather conditions in the middle and northern mainland colonies meant that labor-intensive crops like sugar, rice, and tobacco were not grown there, thus, there was a lesser demand for slave labor.
3. Had it not been for the colonization of the New World in the sixteenth and seventeenth centuries, European enslavement of Africans may have been short-lived and incidental to history. But the discovery of gold and silver and the potential wealth of sugar and tobacco plantations in the Americas created an enormous demand for human labor in the New World. The expanded African slave trade was the response to that demand. Expansion or reduction of colonial territories, occasional moral outrage, disease, harvests, and slaves own procreation all also contributed to ebbs and flows in the slave trade, as did the seventeenth-century law passed in Virginia deeming slaver a materially inheritable condition.
4. The West African source of New World slaves was an area vast enough to contain a large number of cultural groups. Slave traders used this fact to help police their slave cargoes. By selecting each

cargo from several different trading posts on the African coast, slave traders could diminish the ability of their captives to communicate or develop a sense of unity—factors that could potentially contribute to slave mutiny. Once the slaves arrived in the colonies, however, the common experience of slavery slowly dissolved the cultural distinctions between Africans and a common culture emerged.

CHAPTER 5: ANSWERS

THE STRUGGLE FOR THE CONTINENT

READING THE MAP
1. Mississippi
2. New England
3. Quebec and Port Royal (Annapolis Royale)
4. Louisbourg, Cape Breton Island
5. Ft. Duquesne
6. Ft. Duquesne
7. Ft. Niagara

INTERPRETING THE MAP
1. The French colonists, in far fewer numbers than the British, settled in isolated forts along the rivers in the interior of North America. These forts were established primarily to facilitate and protect French fur trading with the Indians and did not threaten the Indians' sovereignty over their tribal lands. In contrast, as builders of agricultural communities, English colonists were constantly seeking land concessions from the Indians.
2. It was a simple matter of proximity. The New England colonies were closer to the major areas of French settlement in New France than were the middle or southern colonies, which rendered them more vulnerable to invasion.
3. Because the southern colonies' profitable rice plantations and fur-trading activities were threatened by raids from Spanish Florida during the colonial wars (Spain was usually an ally of France), the British chartered the Georgia colony as a buffer to protect South Carolina from such raids.

CHAPTER 6: ANSWERS

THE AMERICAN REVOLUTION

READING THE MAP
1. Halifax, Nova Scotia; Halifax
2. Battles fought between British and American troops occurred further east than the Indian battles, which were closer to the trans-Appalachian frontier. American victories there opened the area to rapid settlement after the Revolutionary War.
3. Massachusetts
4. New York, New Jersey, and Pennsylvania

5. North Carolina, South Carolina, and Virginia
6. Except in the Yorktown campaign (where it was critical), their naval strength allowed the British to freely move their troops and supplies along the Atlantic coast.

INTERPRETING THE MAP

1. New York was more centrally located than Boston and it had a superior port. These were important considerations once Britain realized it was going to have to transport large quantities of troops and supplies to America to conduct the war. In addition, because of its location at the mouth of the Hudson River, New York offered a vital staging area for campaigns to the interior.
2. Campaigning in the South was attractive to the British because they could make maximum use of their naval superiority along the lengthy coastline of the southern states and on the navigable rivers to the southern interior.
3. Geographical influences on the conduct of Revolutionary War campaigns included America's vast size, rugged terrain, and distance from Europe. The great distance from Europe hindered British communication and weakened English troops before they arrived in America. The vast interior of North America gave the Americans space to maneuver troops away from pitched battles with the better-trained and professional British army. The British could never station the huge numbers of troops in America that would be necessary to hold this large territory. (And the rugged terrain was an advantage to American troops, who often fought a hit-and-run guerrilla style of warfare, and who learned from the Indians how to benefit from the cover of the woodlands.)

CHAPTER 7: ANSWERS

LAND ACQUISITIONS, 1782–1830

READING THE MAP

1. Virginia
2. Ohio, Appalachian; Ohio, Mississippi
3. 1811 and 1830; 1811 and 1830
4. Mississippi, Rocky
5. Louisiana
6. Spanish, British

INTERPRETING THE MAP

1. The Land Ordinance of 1785 provided for the survey and sale of public lands. This resulted in the more rectangular shape of the new states that entered the Union under its provisions as compared to the original thirteen. It also created a major source of revenue for the federal government. The Ordinance of 1787, called the Northwest Ordinance, provided a framework for the political organization of the territories and their eventual admission to the Union as states. This meant that the nation would avoid the creation of a colonial empire. The Northwest Ordinance also banned slavery from that territory, a precedent that would be the source of great controversy well into the nineteenth century.
2. The Louisiana Purchase, in a single stroke, doubled the size of the United States. It guaranteed the United States free navigation on the Mississippi River, access to the interior, and the use of the port of

New Orleans. All this was vital to the economic development of the trans-Appalachian West. The Purchase also opened a vast new territory for the future growth of the nation—Jefferson's "agrarian republic." But in making the Purchase, the Jeffersonians had to concede the existence of implied powers in the Constitution, a concession that proved to be critically important to the future development and cohesion of the nation.

3. The United States acquired West Florida east to the Pearl River in 1810, when American residents there revolted against Spanish authority and requested annexation by the United States. East Florida was acquired as part of the settlement with Spain in the Adams-Onis Treaty (Transcontinental Treaty) of 1819, which also settled the western boundary of the Louisiana Purchase where is abutted Spanish Texas. The United States established a northern boundary to the Louisiana Purchase when it acquired the Red River Basin (Northern Minnesota and North Dakota) in the Convention of 1818 concluded with Britain. In that same Convention, the United States gained joint occupation rights with Britain to the Oregon Country.

4. Land-use and settlement patterns varied among the different nations colonizing the Americas. Spain's main interest in the New World was to accumulate wealth in the form of gold and silver, so its population not engaged in that was minimal, consisting of missions and a relatively small number of landowners granted large farming tracts by the crown. Likewise, the French were in North America for trade reason and, beyond settlements like Quebec City and Montreal, did not establish much more presence than necessary to protect its trade interests. And after ceding New Amsterdam to the British in the seventeenth century, the Dutch took much the same approach to their remaining outposts in the West Indies. But before that, the Dutch shared with the British an interest in the New World that included, and extended beyond, mere material wealth. Small countries in Europe, to them America offered huge areas of farmland to be exploited in addition to a conveniently removed place to banish undesirables and troublemakers. What all four nations had in common was that they regarded the New World as a colony, never to be the equal of the motherland, and their colonial populations were transient, exiled, or both. In contrast, the Land Ordinance of 1785 aimed to establish permanent communities of Americans by offering land, cheaply, to all white adult male comers and setting aside areas for civic functions like schools. Of course, the way it turned out to work often resembled plantation grants, but it did open the land to settlement and established the precedent for an active Federal role in the westward expansion.

CHAPTER 8: ANSWERS

ROUTES TO THE WEST, 1800–1860

READING THE MAP
1. Lancaster Turnpike (Forbes Road), National Road, and the Hudson–Mohawk Route
2. Cumberland Gap-Road (Wilderness Road)
3. Lancaster Turnpike (Forbes Road); Lancaster Turnpike–Forbes Road–Ohio River route; Cumberland Gap Road–Wilderness Road–Cumberland River
4. Missouri, Yellowstone, and Columbia
5. Mississippi, Arkansas, and Rio Grande
6. Platte, Snake, and Columbia rivers

7. South Pass
8. Platte

INTERPRETING THE MAP

1. Easterners could take the relatively easy routes from the trans-Appalachian West along the Ohio, Wabash, or Tennessee Rivers to the Mississippi River, then travel up the Missouri River to the centrally located settlement at Independence.
2. The Mormons were seeking isolation. They had suffered persecution at the hands of "gentiles" in settled areas in the East and hoped by geographical separation to be able to worship and live according to their own beliefs. In the valley of the Great Salt Lake surrounded by the Wasatch Range, they found arable soil that they successfully irrigated, and there they built a thriving community.
3. The first portion of the Oregon Trail traversed the relatively flat Great Plains. Further westward, however, the pioneers had to cross the Rocky Mountains. Then if they were going to the rich farmland of Oregon, they had to cross the Cascade Mountains, or if their destination was the gold fields of California, they had to cross the Sierra Nevada.
4. Native American groups affected white movement through both hostile and friendly interactions with whites. Native American groups sometimes sheltered, guided, and otherwise assisted the early explorers and trappers. Other times, Native Americans resisted white attempts to "civilize" them and take their lands. Thus Native American groups helped to shape America's westward movement by aiding in the creation of the routes west and through their varying degrees of acquiescence to white settlers influenced which routes would gain popularity.

The introduction of the horse to North America by the Spanish profoundly transformed the cultures of Indians in the plains and Southwest, changing their methods of hunting, traveling, and conducting warfare. But while the horse was assimilated into Native American culture, the changes in the natural environment resulting from white migrations had a deep and almost uniformly negative impact on native peoples. Some groups, such as the Cherokee, had their natural environment resulting from white migrations had a deep and almost uniformly negative impact on native peoples. Some groups such as the Cherokee, had their natural environments forcible changed when the United States confiscated their lands and banished them to barren territories that they were ill-prepared to live on. Others, like the Plains Indians, had their hunting grounds settled by whites and their main source of food, the buffalo, decimated by white hunters.

CHAPTER 9: ANSWERS

THE WAR OF 1812

READING THE MAP

1. Detroit
2. New Orleans

3. Detroit, Buffalo, and Montreal
4. Buffalo, Montreal, Washington, D.C./Baltimore, and New Orleans
5. Chesapeake Bay, Lake Champlain, Lake Erie, Lake Ontario
6. The Thames
7. Horseshoe Bend
8. Chicago

INTERPRETING THE MAP

1. The Battle of New Orleans was a consequence of time and distance. The Treaty of Ghent, ending the War of 1812, was signed on Christmas Eve, 1814, two weeks *before* the Battle of New Orleans. The slowness of communications over the great distance to New Orleans meant that General Jackson and British General Packenham did not hear of the treaty until they had already fought the bloody Battle of New Orleans.
2. Until the very end of the War of 1812, British armies were engaged in the Napoleonic Wars in Europe. Thus, the British navy was dispatched to defend Canada and to blockade the Americans into submission. Thus, the boundary between Canada and the United States east of the Mississippi is a water boundary formed by the Great Lakes and St. Lawrence River, the British employed their naval strength to defend Canada and fight the war.
3. Montreal was the lifeline to England's Canadian settlements further west. By massing forces for the capture of Montreal, rather than dividing them for a multipronged attack on Canada in 1812–1813, the Americans might have gained control of Canada and forced concessions from the British.

CHAPTER 10: ANSWERS

THE MISSOURI COMPROMISE

READING THE MAP

1. 12; 12
2. The Arkansas Territory was open to slavery. The unorganized portion of the old Louisiana Purchase territory north of 36° 30′ N was closed to slavery.
3. Maine
4. The Ohio River
5. 36° 30′ N

INTERPRETING THE MAP

1. The Missouri Compromise dealt with the question of slavery only in the territory acquired in the Louisiana Purchase. Thus, when other territories were added to the Union, the question of slavery expansion had to be debated all over again. This happened when Texas was being considered for annexation in 1845, and again following the acquisition of territories from Mexico in 1848 after the Mexican War.
2. One argument was that the 36° 30′ N line dividing the Louisiana Purchase territory between free and slave areas was a logical extension of the Ohio River line that the Northwest Ordinance used to divide free and slave territories in 1787. It was also argued that by using 36° 30′ N, the new state of Missouri would lie roughly between the same lines of latitude as Virginia, the oldest and most

northerly of the slave states, thus maintaining some geographical symmetry between the free and slave states.

3. The Missouri Compromise gave the North an area of free soil that was many times the size of that allotted to the South. Southern congressmen were willing to vote for this partly because they came to realize that northerners were not going to allow the admission of Missouri as a slave state without this concession. Southerners were also optimistic that the imminent admission of Arkansas and Florida as slave states would give the South a controlling majority in the Senate. This optimism was also based on the belief that the unorganized territory north of 36° 30′ N and west of Missouri was a vast desert suitable only for the Indians and that it would therefore be a very long time before it was ready for free statehood.

CHAPTER 11: ANSWERS

THE ANTEBELLUM SOUTH AND SLAVERY

READING THE MAP

1. South Carolina, Georgia, Florida, Alabama, Mississippi, and Louisiana; The general movement of the slave population was from the Upper South to the Lower South and from the states along the Atlantic Coast west into states along the Gulf of Mexico
2. a. Alabama, Mississippi, Louisiana
   b. South Carolina, Georgia
   c. Virginia, Tennessee

INTERPRETING THE MAP

1. The cotton culture concentrated in areas with the most fertile soils. Southern soil was most fertile in the Black Prairie region of central Alabama and Mississippi and the alluvial lowlands of the lower Mississippi and Red Rivers.
2. The Upper South was generally higher in elevation and had a rougher terrain than the coastal plain of the Lower South. The Upper South also had a lower annual rainfall and it had a shorter growing season (six months) than the Lower South (nine months). These natural features help account for the different kinds of agriculture in the two regions, and thus their economic disparities.
3. The assertion that slavery had reached its natural limits was predicated on the argument that further west from the coastal plain and bottom lands of East Texas, insufficient rainfall prohibited further expansion of the cotton culture. Behind this argument, of course, was the assumption that slavery was uniquely wedded to the cotton culture and would have no utility where cotton could not grow.

CHAPTER 12: ANSWERS

SETTLING THE BOUNDARY WITH CANADA

READING THE MAP

1. 49th (49° N latitude)

2. Willamette and Columbia
3. Vancouver Island
4. Maine and New Hampshire
5. Lake of the Woods and Lake Superior

INTERPRETING THE MAP

1. The Oregon Settlement gave the United States possession of the Columbia River and of Puget Sound. The latter was desired for its value to the future of American trade from the Pacific Coast to Asian markets. President Polk, a Southerner, also though the Oregon Country unfit for agriculture and any states formed from it would thus be unsympathetic to slavery. Less area likely would mean fewer states.
2. Lying below the boundary line drawn would be in the Webster-Ashburton Treaty was the Mesabi Range in northern Minnesota Territory, a fabulously rich store of iron ore. Undiscovered at the time of the treaty, this rich source of iron ore would be of great value to America's industrialization in the late nineteenth century.
3. The British wanted to build a military road from St. John to Quebec. The proposed road would run through territory that had been in dispute between Canada and Maine since 1783. So that the British might build their road and the boundary might be peacefully established, the United States and Britain negotiated the Webster-Ashburton Treaty in 1842. The United States received just over half of the disputed territory.

CHAPTER 13: ANSWERS

TEXAS AND THE MEXICAN WAR

READING THE MAP

1. Sabine; Arkansas; Red; Rio Grande
2. Rio Grande; Gila
3. 42nd parallel (42° N latitude)
4. Nueces River, Rio Grande
5. Santa Fe; California
6. Vera Cruz; Mexico City

INTERPRETING THE MAP

1. California had a long Pacific coastline and two natural harbors, San Francisco and San Diego. By acquiring California, the United States improved its navy's strategic position and increased the opportunities for American merchants to compete with the British for trade with Asia.
2. As Americans discovered, even as the Treaty of Guadeloupe Hidalgo was being completed, California was rich with gold. Later, enormous wealth in gold and silver was mined out of other parts of the Cession Territory; the territory was also rich in industrial ores—zinc, copper, and bauxite among them. Along with Texas, California also became a major source of petroleum. All these natural resources acquired from Mexico in 1848 contributed to the modernization and wealth of the American economy.

3. Missing from this map is the 30 million acres of territory acquired from Mexico in 1853 via the Gadsden Purchase. James Gadsden, from South Carolina and the American minister to Mexico, negotiated the purchase of the strip of territory in the Masilla Valley lying just south of the Gila River. The $10 million purchase was made so that a transcontinental railroad to southern California could be built. The Gadsden Purchase territory is now the southernmost portions of Arizona and New Mexico.

CHAPTER 14: ANSWERS

THE COMPROMISE OF 1850 AND THE KANSAS-NEBRASKA ACT

READING THE MAP
1. 36° 30′ N; 42° N; 49° N
2. In 1850, the nation was divided roughly evenly between slave and free. With the application of popular sovereignty to Kansas-Nebraska Territory, the slave states and territories open to slavery comprised a larger area than the free states and territories.
3. Canada (49° N); Rocky Mountains (Continental Divide); Indian Territory(36° 30′ N); Missouri River and the state of Missouri
4. California

INTERPRETING THE MAP
1. Missouri's interest in slavery being permitted in Kansas was a matter of proximity and the security of slave property. Kansas Territory would lie directly west of Missouri. If Kansas were banned to slavery and became a free state, Missouri would be a slave state bounded on three sides by free states (Illinois, Iowa, and Kansas). It was argued that this would make it relatively easy for slaves to escape from Missouri, and thus diminish the value of slave property in the state.
2. Some, including Senator Douglas, believed that the Kansas-Nebraska Territory was inhospitable to slavery since it lay too far north to support cotton farming. But, by 1854, northerners no longer trusted this "natural limits" argument and came to see the southern "Slave Power" as aggressively bent on the expansion of slaveholding interests and asserting southern control of the federal government. They were infuriated by the South's eagerness to repeal the Missouri Compromise's ban on slavery north of 36° 30′ N latitude.
3. Although the portion of the old Louisiana Purchase that remained unorganized into the 1850s was widely viewed as an inhospitable dessert, there was nevertheless considerable interest in it from both the North and South, as well as from commercial interests. Railroad interests were eager to lay tracks across the continent, which would stimulate settlement in the territory. Such construction and settlement required Indian removal and surveying of the land, and thus some sort of political organization of this territory because they saw it as a means by which they could increase their strength in Congress relative to the other, depending on whether the states formed there entered the Union as slave or free.
4. The states that joined the Confederacy were all united by, among other things, their economic dependence on labor-intensive, plantation-system agriculture, primarily rice and cotton farming. Their environments were well suited to these crops. The slave states remaining in the Union, for the

most, part did not share this environment and thus did not develop economies so heavily dependent on the slave-labor plantation system.

CHAPTER 15: ANSWERS

THE SECCESSION CRISIS

READING THE MAP

1. 15
2. Missouri, Kentucky, Maryland, and Delaware
3. Ohio River
4. Arkansas, Louisiana, and Texas
5. Montgomery, Alabama; Richmond, Virginia

INTERPRETING THE MAP

1. Texas bordered on Mexico, which meant that when the Union navy blockaded the Confederate coast it was still possible for the Confederacy to gain access to foreign goods that could be shipped to Mexico, then carted over the Rio Grande into Texas and on to the eastern Confederacy. Confederate Texas also deprived the Union of a large western staging ground for attacks on the Lower South.
2. By not joining the Confederacy, Missouri and Kentucky guaranteed the Union's control of the Ohio and upper Mississippi Rivers. These were major transportation arteries and the Union movement of troops and supplies would have been severely hindered had they been in Confederate hands. Maryland's decision not to secede meant that Washington, D.C., on the Maryland-Virginia border, would not be surrounded by Confederate territory.
3. There is a close correlation between the three tiers and the proportion of slaves in their total population. The Lower South, from South Carolina and Georgia across the Gulf Coast to Texas, was the land of King Cotton, where slavery was most vital to economic health. (Slaves comprised over 40 percent of the population in each of these states.) In the middle tier of Arkansas, Tennessee, North Carolina, and Virginia, slaves were declining in numbers as these economies became more diversified. (The slave proportion of the total population in these states ranged from 23 percent in Tennessee to 39 percent in Virginia.) Those slave states that remained loyal to the Union had the lowest percentage of slaves in their population of all the slave states (from 2 percent in Delaware to 23 percent in Maryland).

CHAPTER 16: ANSWERS

THE CIVIL WÀR

READING THE MAP

1. Richmond; James; York
2. Gettysburg, Pennsylvania, and Antietam, Maryland
3. Mississippi; Tennessee; Atlanta to Savannah, Georgia

4. New Orleans; Vicksburg, Mississippi
5. Henry and Donelson; Shiloh, Tennessee
6. Railroads, weapons, numbers of soldiers. Geographical size, leadership, tacit support of European allies.

INTERPRETING THE MAP

1. The location of the capital cities of the two sides, Washington, D.C., and Richmond, Virginia, are only about 100 miles apart. Both sides had to mass and maintain sizable armies to defend their respective capitals. The capture of Richmond was one of the three strategic objectives of the Union war plan.
2. Western Tennessee, where the Cumberland and Tennessee Rivers flow from south to north into the Ohio River, was an opening to the South for Union armies. Tennessee was also strategically important as a granary for the Confederacy, and Chattanooga, along with Atlanta, Georgia, was a major hub of southern railroad transportation.
3. The Confederacy had over 3,000 miles of coastline. Even with its naval superiority, the Union navy was stretched too thin to ever completely blockade all Confederate ports. Blockade running was a highly profitable enterprise for Confederate entrepreneurs.
4. At the time of the Civil War, the North was far ahead of the south in its industrialization and transportation network. With the South's few industrial sites concentrated in its important cities like Richmond and Charleston, and its railroad hub in Atlanta, the North had relatively easy targets. Likewise, by concentrating their efforts on conquering Mississippi ports like Vicksburg and New Orleans, the North could cripple Southern river transportation and cut off the Southern interiors direct access to the Atlantic and Gulf of Mexico. By contrast, even if the Confederacy had decided to pursue an offensive strategy in the war, the North's complex systems of roads, rails, canal, and rivers, as well as its multiple, geographically diversified industrial centers and ports, would have made disabling the North a most difficult proposition.

CHAPTER 17: ANSWERS

RAILROADS AND THE NEW TRANSPORTATION SYSTEMS

READING THE MAP

1. Omaha, Sacramento
2. Promontory Point, Salt Lake City, Utah
3. Southern Pacific Railroad
4. China; Ireland

INTERPRETING THE MAP

1. The opening of the transcontinental railroad helped to usher the American economy into an era of explosive growth. Both merchants and farmers found national markets for their goods; with the railroad, people and goods could move throughout the country more quickly, conveniently, and eventually more cheaply, than ever before, and farmers could get their crops and livestock to market more easily. As the railroads shaped the economy, they also shaped American society by helping to populate the West and pulling people closer together: the railroads connected the coasts with each

other and with the interior of the country physically and metaphorically. The society of the West began to resemble that of the rest of the country.

2. The railroads influenced the settlement and development patterns of the United States in much the same way that explorers and their routes had in an earlier era. People settled in railroad hubs or along the railroad lines; farmers located themselves in proximity to depots from which they could shop their produce to market.

3. The transcontinental railroad ran up against the same natural hurdles that faced the wagon trains of the early nineteenth century: the Rocky Mountains, then the Sierra Nevada on the way to California and the Cascade Mountains into the Pacific Northwest, in addition to many desert areas, rivers, and hostile Indian tribes along the way. Social and political hurdles were substantial also. The railroads literally put towns on the map and very often delivered economic growth; thus, enticing a railroad to come through one's town was a goal of many western politicians. However, this increased economic activity included the businesses that serviced a transient population of railroad workers and gamblers: not only provisions and inns, but also saloons and brothels. Moral crusaders of the nineteenth century say (particularly in Utah) saw these as pernicious influences on American society and at times fought the railroads on those grounds.

4. Among the many ways that the railroad altered the environment of the West was its bringing waves of settlers and prospectors to previously unpopulated or sparsely populated lands. And because they made for faster access to larger markets, the railroads allowed farmers to put more land into cultivation. The railroads also, through the ever-popular bison hunt, contributed to the extermination of those animals and the Native American groups that depended on them for food.

CHAPTER 18: ANSWERS

TERRITORIAL EXPANSION TO THE CIVIL WAR

READING THE MAP

1. New Hampshire, Massachusetts, Connecticut, Rhode Island, New York, New Jersey, Pennsylvania, Delaware, Maryland, Virginia, North Carolina, South Carolina, Georgia
2. Ohio, Indiana, Illinois, Michigan, Wisconsin, (and Minnesota)
3. Kentucky, Tennessee, Alabama, Mississippi, Vermont, and Maine
4. Louisiana, Arkansas, Missouri, Iowa, North Dakota, South Dakota, Nebraska, Kansas, Oklahoma, Colorado, Wyoming, and Montana
5. Florida
6. Texas was annexed directly to statehood from it status as the independent Lone Star Republic. The territory claimed by Texas when it was annexed also include what are now portions of the states of New Mexico, Oklahoma, Kansas, Colorado, and Wyoming.
7. California, Nevada, Utah, Arizona, New Mexico, Colorado, and Wyoming
8. Washington, Oregon, Idaho, Montana, and Wyoming

INTERPRETING THE MAP

1. Pushing Native Americans further westward ahead of the American transcontinental movement affected the development of the West in many ways. For a few, it meant that certain areas would be ostensibly off-limits to settlements as they were traditional Indian lands or reservations, that life on

the frontier would be dangerous and lived under the threat of Indian attack, and that the U.S. military would have a role in the settlement of the continent, as they were often needed to move Indians off lands, to establish American outposts on the frontier, and to protect settlers.

2. There are many possible answers to the question. A correctly formulated answer should be detailed and focus on one aspect of differences and distinctions.

CHAPTER 19: ANSWERS

RECONSTRUCTION

READING THE MAP

1. Tennessee
2. Tennessee
3. Virginia and Georgia
4. South Carolina, Florida, and Louisiana
5. Virginia
6. North Carolina, South Carolina, Tennessee, Florida, Alabama, Arkansas, Louisiana
7. South Carolina, Florida, and Louisiana

INTERPRETING THE MAP

1. The former Confederate states were divided into military districts, each governed by an army general, as a way of maintaining law and order in the region and establishing an administrative shell under which the states could take the steps mandated by Congress for readmission.
2. Federal troops still occupied the capitals of South Carolina and Louisiana when the 1876 election was held. The so-called Compromise of 1877 allegedly included a promise by Republican candidate Rutherford B. Hayes to withdraw these troops if the Democrats assented to his election.
3. In observance of states' rights, each former Confederate state was required to draft its own state constitution and elect state officers that would satisfy congressional readmission requirements. The time it took to do this varied from state to state.

Page References

Chapter 1: The Physical and Political Setting

	Martin, et. al. *America and Its Peoples*, 3/e	Nash/Jeffrey, *The American People*, 4/e	Divine, et. al. *America Past and Present*, 4/e	Wilson, et. al. *Pursuit of Liberty*, 3/e	Garraty, *The American Nation*, 9/e
Mapping America				—	
Question 1.	front endpaper	226, 281	rear endpaper	—	13, 25, 62, 317
Question 2.	front endpaper	281	rear endpaper	—	13, 25, 62, 173, 231, 317
Question 3.	front endpaper	—	rear endpaper	—	—
Reading the Map					
Question 1.	front endpaper	—	350, rear endpaper	—	317
Question 2.	front endpaper	438	xxx, rear endpaper	—	209, 231
Question 3.	front endpaper	438	xxx, rear endpaper	—	231
Question 4.	front endpaper	—	rear endpaper	—	317
Question 5.	front endpaper	226	238, rear endpaper	—	231
Question 6.	front endpaper	—	rear endpaper	—	126
Question 7.	front endpaper	—	rear endpaper	—	475
Question 8.	front endpaper	463	rear endpaper	—	475
Question 9.	front endpaper	—	rear endpaper	—	—
Interpreting the Map					
Question 1.	front endpaper	281, 288–89, 432–69	rear endpaper	—	13, 25, 62, 173, 226, 231, 314–18
Question 2.	front endpaper	—	rear endpaper	—	—
Question 3.	—	111–12, 281, 330, 433–36, 445–52	20, 99–105, 228–29, 260–71, 343–50	68–86	37–43, 44–45, 48, 226, 314–18, 464–77
Question 4.	5–11	8–9, 105–8, 461–64	2–6	24–27, 154–55	9–13, 460–64
Question 5.	28–29	105–8, 149, 461–64	6–8, 10–11	33, 42–44, 154–55	9–13, 248–49
Question 6.	front endpaper, 199	223, 463	rear endpaper, 177–80, 344	—	124–25, 475

Chapter 2: Discovery and Exploration

	Martin, et. al.	Nash/Jeffrey	Divine, et. al.	Wilson, et. al.	Garraty
Mapping America					
Question 1.	front & rear endpaper, 81	16, 24	rear endpaper	32	7, 10
Question 2.	424, 439, 705	24	106	9, 32, 39	
Question 3.	11, 17	—	17	—	7
Question 4.	rear endpaper	16	rear endpaper	9	7
Question 5.	17	16	17	32	7
Question 6.	11	14	5	—	13
Reading the Map					

Question 1.	15	19	—	—	7
Question 2.	17, 21	21	—	—	7
Question 3.	17, 21	30	17	29	13
Question 4.	17, 21	21	17	31, 32	13
Question 5.	17, 19	16	17	32	7, 9
Question 6.	104	16, 94	17, 20	116	7
Question 7.	19	24	—	30	8
Question 8.	16	23	17	—	30
Question 9.	17–18	24	17, 18	29–30	8, 11
Question 10.	17	28	—	—	—
Interpreting the Map					
Question 1.	rear endpaper, 14, 15	16	rear endpaper	9, 28–32	7
Question 2.	16	23	17	—	—
Question 3.	—	—	—	9	—
Question 4.	4–34	25–26, 105–8, 115–16	10–11	33–34, 68–86	7, 9–10, 28–30

Chapter 3: England's North American Colonies in 1700

	Martin, et. al.	Nash/Jeffrey	Divine, et. al.	Wilson, et. al.	Garraty
Mapping America					
Question 1.	front endpaper, 82	59	xxvii, 50, 51, 103	—	39, 50, 61
Question 2.	front endpaper, 31, 45, 57, 90, 280	41, 59	35, 50, 51, 103	85, 115, 129, 161	39, 50, 61
Question 3.	front endpaper, 45, 58	41, 59	35, 50, 51, rear endpaper	—	39, 50, 61
Question 4.	58, 85–86, 105	82–85, 94	82–84, 121, 122–23	123–25, 316–17	10, 43, 80
Question 5.	11, 31, 79	14	5	39	13
Reading the Map					
Question 1.	45	59	103	—	39
Question 2.	82	41, 59	51, 103	—	50
Question 3.	82	59	51, 103	—	61
Question 4.	—	41, 59	103	—	50
Question 5.	31–32, 45	38, 52	34–35	40–41	16, 39
Question 6.	106	59	58, 103	134–151	47–48
Question 7.	82	59	51, 103	—	61
Interpreting the Map					
Question 1.	57	41, 59, 121–22	35, 50–51, 103	68–86, 129	39, 50, 61
Question 2.	—	36–97	34–60, 106–7	117–22	25, 69–74
Question 3.	58–70	36–97, 111–21	34–60, 64–82	68–86	36–63
Question 4.	93	—	42–50, 103	—	—

Chapter 4: The Atlantic Slave Trade

	Martin, et. al.	Nash/Jeffrey	Divine, et. al.	Wilson, et. al.	Garraty, et. al.
Mapping America					
Question 1.	rear endpaper, 69	74	9, 74, 106	115	41
Question 2.	rear endpaper, 69	—	74, rear endpaper	115	41
Question 3.	—	—	—	—	—
Question 4.	—	—	9	115	—
Question 5.	—	—	9	—	—
Reading the Map					
Question 1.	—	73	12	—	—

	Martin, et. al.	Nash/Jeffrey	Divine, et. al.	Wilson, et. al.	Garraty
Question 2.	—	—	—	—	—
Question 3.	—	—	9, 74, rear endpaper	—	—
Question 4.	91	73	—	—	—
Question 5.	—	78	—	—	—
Interpreting the Map					
Question 1.	rear endpaper, 17	72–73	12	28, 115	6
Question 2.	—	74–76	73–79	115, 150	41
Question 3.	20, 40–41, 42,66–70	72–76	73–79	115, 150	39–41, 44–45
Question 4.	68–70	74–80	73–79	—	—

Chapter 5: The Struggle for the Continent

	Martin, et. al.	Nash/Jeffrey	Divine, et. al.	Wilson, et. al.	Garraty
Mapping America					
Question 1.	front endpaper	152	rear endpaper	—	83
Question 2.	109	—	57, 120, 126	85–161	83
Question 3.	81	152	xxviii, 120, 178	171	86
Question 4.	118	152	127	171	86
Reading the Map					
Question 1.	104, 108	94, 107, 147	20, 120–26	168	—
Question 2.	105	94, 96, 147–50	120–26	168	81
Question 3.	109	94, 150	120–26	168	83
Question 4.	106	149	125	—	83
Question 5.	108	148	126	—	83
Question 6.	108	149	124	—	81–82
Question 7.	—	149	125	169	82
Interpreting the Map					
Question 1.	104–5	57–58, 107, 148	20, 120–21	37–38	—
Question 2.	82, 105	95, 96	120–27	—	81, 83
Question 3.	106	110	58–60	134–151	47–48, 86

Chapter 6: The American Revolution

	Martin, et. al.	Nash/Jeffrey	Divine, et. al	Wilson, et. al.	Garraty
Mapping America					
Question 1.	163	185	126, 156, 157	161–207	115
Question 2.	163, 173	185, 188	156, 157, 160	207	105, 112, 115
Question 3.	121	152	127, 138	171	86
Question 4.	190	226	xxix, 154, 178	236	126
Reading the Map					
Question 1.	163	183	156, 157	—	109
Question 2.	169–71	189–91	—	208	—
Question 3.	151–52, 156–57	165, 169	150	202–3	103
Question 4.	163, 164–72	182, 183–84	156–57	206–10	111–12
Question 5.	173, 175–78	182, 186–89	159–60	207, 210–12	115
Question 6.	—	182	153	206	—
Interpreting the Map					
Question 1.	162, 163	183	155	204	109
Question 2.	172–73	186	159	210–12	113–14
Question 3.	162–78	183–84, 186–89	153	202–12	103–4, 105–6. 111–14

Chapter 7: Land Acquisitions, 1782–1830

	Martin, et. al.	Nash/Jeffrey	Divine, et. al.	Wilson, et. al.	Garraty
Mapping America					
Question 1.	190, 204, 253, 264, 275	187, 226, 281	xxx, 178, 238, 261, 265	171, 236, 257, 285, 359	126, 173
Question 2.	front endpaper	226, 281	178, rear endpaper	—	126
Reading the Map					
Question 1.	190		178	—	126
Question 2.	264	292, 463	178	—	248–50
Question 3.	—	289–95	262–64, 265	—	—
Question 4.	253	281	238	284, 285	173
Question 5.	251–52, 253	277–78, 281	238	284, 285	132
Question 6.	253	281	238	285	173
Interpreting the Map					
Question 1.	199	223	177–79	235	125
Question 2.	251–52	277–78	237–39	284, 85	167–69
Question 3.	279	278	261, 344	354	196–97
Question 4.	19–20, 32–33, 41–43, 199	26–28, 40–41, 54, 57–60, 223	14–20, 34–61, 103, 105–7, 177–79	34–40, 68–86, 235	8–9, 24–28, 36–42, 44–45, 47–48, 125

Chapter 8: Routes to the West, 1800–1860

	Martin, et. al.	Nash/Jeffrey	Divine, et. al.	Wilson, et. al.	Garraty
Mapping America					
Question 1.	front endpaper, 424	291, 451	178, 350, rear endpaper	499	317
Question 2.	front endpaper, 424	291, 451	350, rear endpaper	499	231, 317
Question 3.	199, 424	451	272, 350	499	231, 317
Question 4.	253	281	238	285	173
Question 5.	314	—	265	—	250
Reading the Map					
Question 1.	—	288	—	—	231
Question 2.	—	—	—	—	231
Question 3.	—	—	272	—	—
Question 4.	front endpaper, 253	280, 281	238	285	173
Question 5.	421	280, 281	—	285	173
Question 6.	424	451	350	499	317
Question 7.	424	451	350	499	317
Question 8.	front endpaper	451	350, rear endpaper	499	317
Interpreting the Map					
Question 1.	425	450, 451	350	499	—
Question 2.	front endpaper, 435	457–58	349–50	413	272
Question 3.	425–26	450–51	349	499	—
Question 4.	229–30, 312–15, 417–19, 552–57	461–65	202–65, 299–301, 506–13	70, 168, 155–56, 323–27, 487	186, 249–50, 460–64

Chapter 9: The War of 1812

	Martin, et. al.	Nash/Jeffrey	Divine, et. al.	Wilson, et. al.	Garraty
Mapping America					

Question 1.	front endpaper, 259	310	rear endpaper	288–89	—
Question 2.	front endpaper, 259	310	252, rear endpaper	288–89	—
Reading the Map					
Question 1.	259	310	252	—	190
Question 2.	259, 261	308, 310	252	289	193
Question 3.	259	—	252	287, 289	190
Question 4.	259, 260	—	252	288	191
Question 5.	259, 260	308, 310	252, 253	287–89	190, 191
Question 6.	260	—	—	—	186, 190
Question 7.	—	—	—	—	—
Question 8.	259	310	252	—	—
Interpreting the Map					
Question 1.	259, 261	310	252, 253	289	193–94
Question 2.	258–61	310	252	287–89	—
Question 3.	259	310	252	288, 289	190

Chapter 10: The Missouri Compromise

	Martin, et. al.	Nash/Jeffrey	Divine, et. al.	Wilson, et. al.	Garraty
Mapping America					
Question 1.	294	314	265, 281, rear endpaper	368	209
Question 2.	294	314	281	368	209
Question 3.	294	314	281	368	209
Reading the Map					
Question 1.	294	314	281	368	209
Question 2.	294	313, 314	281	367–68	208, 209
Question 3.	294	313	281	367–68	208
Question 4.	front endpaper, 294	312, 314	281, rear endpaper	—	208, 209
Question 5.	294	313, 314	281	367–68	208, 209
Interpreting the Map					
Question 1.	294	313, 314	280, 281	367–68	209
Question 2.	—	—	280, 281	—	—
Question 3.	front endpaper, 294	314	280, 281	368	208, 209

Chapter 11: The Antebellum South and Slavery

	Martin, et. al.	Nash/Jeffrey	Divine, et. al	Wilson, et. al.	Garraty
Mapping America					
Question 1.	453	362	381	443, 455	338
Question 2.	380	365	377, 375	—	338
Question 3.	453		381	443, 455	
Reading the Map					
Question 1.	454	360, 362	381	455	338
Question 2.	380, 454	362, 365	272, 377, 380	—	338
Question 3.	453, 454	361–64	380, 381	—	225, 338
Interpreting the Map					
Question 1.	front endpaper, 454	361–65	375–77	320–23, 443–45	—
Question 2.	front endpaper, 380, 454	365	rear endpaper	320–23, 443–45	335–44
Question 3.	front endpaper, 380	365	rear endpaper	—	328

Chapter 12: Settling the Boundary with Canada

	Martin, et. al.	Nash/Jeffrey	Divine, et. al.	Wilson, et. al.	Garraty
Mapping America					
Question 1.	420	438	309, 344	443, 491	331
Question 2.	420, 432	444	355, rear endaper	491	331
Question 3.	420	—	344	—	331
Question 4.	432	444	355	491	331
Reading the Map					
Question 1.	432	444	354–55	491	319
Question 2.	424	444	350	491	317
Question 3.	432	444	354–55	491	319, 331
Question 4.	420	—	344	—	331
Question 5.	431	—	—	—	331
Interpreting the Map					
Question 1.	432–33	444	354	490	319
Question 2.	420	—	—	—	—
Question 3.	420, 431	—	343	—	312

Chapter 13: Texas and the Mexican War

	Martin, et. al.	Nash/Jeffrey	Divine, et. al.	Wilson, et. al.	Garraty
Mapping America					
Question 1.	front endpaper, 432, 439	439	347, 357	493, 499	322
Question 2.	front endpaper, 439	439, 443	347, 357	493	322
Question 3.	420	438	357	489	322
Question 4.	420, 439	438	357	499	331
Question 5.	439	443	357	492–93	322
Reading the Map					
Question 1.	front endpaper, 420	438, 439	357	493	322
Question 2.	front endpaper, 420	438	357	—	331
Question 3.	432	444	355, 357	—	—
Question 4.	439	440, 443	355, 357	490, 493	320
Question 5.	438, 439	442, 443	356, 357	492–93	322
Question 6.	438, 439	443	356, 357	493	322
Interpreting the Map					
Question 1.	436–37	442	358	490	—
Question 2.	front endpaper, 420	438	356–58	—	324
Question 3.	420, 467	438, 484	358	498, 499	331, 366

Chapter 14: The Compromise of 1850 and the Kansas–Nebraska Act

	Martin, et. al.	Nash/Jeffrey	Divine, et. al.	Wilson, et. al.	Garraty
Mapping America					
Question 1.	294, 432, 468	314, 444, 478, 502	281, 355, 408	499, 500	331
Question 2.	468	478	408	500	330, 365–67
Reading the Map					
Question 1.	291–95, 468, 455–57	314	281, 408	367–68, 443, 498, 499, 500	208–9, 327–30, 365–66
Question 2.	468	478, 502	408	500	330, 365–66

Question 3.	front endpaper, 468	502	408	498, 499, 500	380
Question 4.	455–57	475	406, 408	496, 500	329
Interpreting the Map					
Question 1.	468, 470–72	488, 502	408	500	380
Question 2.	front endpaper, 468, 470–72	482–83	410	498–500	366–67
Question 3.	467–70	482	409	498	365–66
Question 4.	front endpaper, 380, 490	365, 490–92, 497	377, 381, 444	320–22, 443, 529	338, 383

Chapter 15: The Secession Crisis

	Martin, et. al.	Nash/Jeffrey	Divine, et. al.	Wilson, et. al.	Garraty
Mapping America					
Question 1.	front endpaper, 498	365, 511, 514,	444, 446, rear endpaper	529	383
Question 2.	490	511	444	529	383
Question 3.	490	478, 511	444	529	330, 383
Reading the Map					
Question 1.	490	475, 478	444	529	380
Question 2.	490	478, 511	444	529	330, 383
Question 3.	front endaper, 490	511	444	—	383
Question 4.	490	511	444	529	383
Question 5.	489, 495	—	440, 443	531	381, 390
Interpreting the Map					
Question 1.	490	507, 511	444	529	383
Question 2.	491–92	507–8	443–44	529	330, 383
Question 3.	454, 490	365, 366	440, 444	—	338

Chapter 16: The Civil War

	Martin, et. al.	Nash/Jeffrey	Divine, et. al.	Wilson, et. al.	Garraty
Mapping America					
Question 1.	498, 513	513, 514, 524	453, 455, 462, 463, 465	532, 533, 534, 535, 543, 546, 547, 548	394, 396, 403, 410
Question 2.	front endpaper	513, 514, 524	rear endpaper, 446, 453, 455	532, 533, 534, 547	356, 394, 396, 410
Question 3.	513	524	465	547	—
Question 4.	280–83, 380	325, 451	350, 360, 363–63	499	231, 317, 356
Reading the Map					
Question 1.	499	512–13	453, 455	534	395, 396
Question 2.	498, 513	513, 524	455, 462	534, 535, 542–44	396, 397, 403
Question 3.	496, 516–18	513–14, 524–25	463–64, 465	531, 546, 547	394–95, 408–9
Question 4.	498, 500–501	515, 524	453, 461–62	533	394, 403–5
Question 5.	498, 500	514	452, 453	—	394, 395
Question 6.	491–95	507	444–47	530–31	388–89
Interpreting the Map					
Question 1.	498	508, 511	446	532, 534	396
Question 2.	498, 500–501	513–14	452–53	533	—
Question 3.	497	515	446	531	383, 388–89
Question 4.	280–83, 377–79, 380, 382–83, 393–95, 397–98, 493, 516–18	507	447	530	356, 388–89

Chapter 17: Railroads and New Transportation Systems

	Martin, et. al.	Nash/Jeffrey	Divine, et. al.	Wilson, et. al. (v. II)	Garraty
Mapping America					
Question 1.	—	—	—	—	231
Question 2.	—	619	540	151	475
Question 3.	front endpaper	325, 619	rear endpaper,	151	356, 475
Question 4.	380	451	523, 531	151	475
Reading the Map					
Question 1.	—	619	541	146, 151	471–72, 475
Question 2.	—	619	542	147, 151	473, 475
Question 3.	—	619	543	151	471–72, 475
Question 4.	—	626	542	146, 147	472
Interpreting the Map					
Question 1.	568–69	323, 578–89	526–31	146–51	464–75
Question 2.	568–69, 586–87	323, 578–89	538–45	146–51	470–73, 476
Question 3.	front endpaper, 504, 558, 568–69, 572, 581	—	540–45	151	470–73
Question 4.	568–69, 572, 581, 586–87	578–89	532, 537–543	146–59	470–73

Chapter 18: Territorial Expansion to the Civil War

	Martin, et. al.	Nash/Jeffrey	Divine, et. al.	Wilson, et. al.	Garraty
Mapping America					
Question 1.	190, 420	438	xxviii, xxix, xxx 344	257, 285, 354, 489, 499	126, 198, 331
Question 2.	554	592	509	II.134	462
Reading the Map					
Question 1.	190	438	xxxii	245, 257	126
Question 2.	190, 420	438	xxxiii, 344	257, 500	126, 198, 331
Question 3.	190, 420	438	xxxiii, 344	257, 500	126, 331
Question 4.	420	438	344	285, 529	167, 475
Question 5.	420	278	344	354	197, 198
Question 6.	420, 430–31	438, 440	346–48	490	331
Question 7.	420	438, 442–43	344	499	331
Question 8.	420	438, 443–44	344	499	331
Interpreting the Map					
Question 1.	229–30, 307, 312–15, 417–19, 552–57, 582–83	289–95, 404–5, 461–64, 589–95596	506–13	151–56	460–62, 464
Question 2.	419–27, 430–35, 580–81, 584–87, 662–68	280–89, 351–56, 452–61, 578–89, 605–11	526–32	157–59	459, 468–77, 513–14

Chapter 19: Reconstruction

	Martin, et. al.	Nash/Jeffrey	Divine, et. al.	Wilson, et. al.	Garraty
Mapping America					
Question 1.	547	—	497	—	426
Question 2.	547	563	497	592	426
Reading the Map					

Question 1.	547	563, 570	497	592	424, 426
Question 2.	547	563, 570	497	592	424
Question 3.	547	563	497	592	426
Question 4.	547	563, 570	497	592	426
Question 5.	547	563	497	592	426
Question 6.	547	563	497	592	426
Question 7.	547	563, 570	497	592	426
Interpreting the Map					
Question 1.	—	550	—	583	424
Question 2.	—	—	496	—	439
Question 3.	538	550	479	583, 586–87	424